"What is a life well lived? To ask that question is to have the greatest courage to reflect and self-examine. Aldo traces his life's story from early childhood in Cuba, through the trials of his young exile from his native country, and to the tests of building and continually re-building and re-inventing his life in the U.S.. His powerful emotional journey stirs up our deepest fears as we find out how, because of the threats of the Communist regime in Cuba, his parents decide to send him to the U.S. knowing they might never see him again. His parent's greatest sacrifice is made in the name of saving the child's life – it emerges from and is sustained by the unspoken gift of unconditional love, the very sustenance of life itself."

Ljudmila Mila Popovich, poet and critical writer
Author of Cinemagic Realism: Magic Realisim in
International Cinema

"The Unspoken Gift is a wonderful story which should be an inspiration to all who have the pleasure of reading it. Aldo's strong sense of family and community, and his dedication to both, as well as his sense of humor, shine through every page in this enlightening book. Those who read this book will find Aldo to be a mentor and friend in their professional and personal lives through his story. Enjoy!"

Judy Bryngil Treston
Former vice president of the New York Stock Exchange

"Some people forger coal from their life's experiences; Aldo Martinez forged diamonds."

Frank Kerr
Retired Businessman

Years ago James Barrie wrote about Peter Pan and his adventurous flights at night. In The Unspoken Gift, Aldo Martinez tells about his adventures as a Pedro Pan child after he flew out of Cuba in a twin engine plane on February 6, 1962, at the age of 11. Martinez recognized early that education was necessary for his success and completed college and Law School. His ability to work in a job he enjoyed and to rise through the ranks at the New York Stock Exchange to become the Managing director at age 37 and the only Hispanic Vice President at the age of 39, is another example of his success. His love for family is rooted in his parents' love for him and their sacrifice to give him a better life by sending him to America. Martinez demonstrates that no matter where someone is born, if a person strives for success, his dreams will be fulfilled.

Sr. Dorothy Jehle, OP
Professor Emeritus & former director of archives,
Msgr. Wlm. Barry Memorial Library
Barry University,
Miami, Florida

The

Unspoken

Gift

How an Immigrant Cuban Child Fulfilled His American Dream

By
Aldo Martinez

Cover Photo by Aldo Martinez, Jr.

Open Door Publications

The Unspoken Gift:
How an Immigrant Cuban Child
Fulfilled His American Dream

Published by
Open Door Publications
27 Carla Way
Lawrenceville, NJ 08648
www.OpenDoorPublications.com

Cover Photo, photo of the author and some additional
photos by Aldo Martinez, Jr.

Cover Design by Jessica Chao

ISBN: 978-0-9838750-4-8

DEDICATION

I dedicate this book to my family, who has been part of my soul and responsible for giving me the love I have needed to have the courage to choose to live. We all have amazing stories to tell. My journey is a story of personal, professional and family triumphs; it is an imperfect journey through darkness surrendering to love in order to treasure life's challenges and uncertainties. My journey is not over, and it will not end until my last breath.

I dedicate these words to my wife, Susan, whose love has filled and fueled me and without whom I may not have been able to experience the peacefulness of true happiness. To Christine, Danielle, Aldo and Melissa, my children, for whom these lines have been written and who not only have taught me so much about love but who, by being themselves, I have grown to value and respect their judgment and conduct. To Simon and Samantha, my grandchildren, Christine's children who have already given me the gift of feeling the joy that my grandfather felt when he shared my childhood moments, and to my brother, Carlos (Migue), who has also traveled a journey through darkness and has triumphed and now lives his dream. Christine, Danielle and Migue share their dreams with their spouses, Brian, Greg and Toni Ann, respectively.

Finally, to my mom and dad who gave me the unspoken gift of love without which nothing of what has happened in my life would have been possible. I dedicate this book to all of them for giving me the greatest gift of all: love.

Table of Contents

INTRODUCTION

My first memories are of bars. The ornate bars that decorate the windows and doors of many of the homes in Cuba, where I was born, are intricate and beautiful in design. But no matter how attractive bars appear, they imprison us in life. I became a prisoner of circumstances that I could not control: a dysfunctional family, a political regime that brought me face to face with death and separation from loved ones. As I grew older, these bars turned into cultural, language and ethnic barriers: prejudice that was sometimes subtle and at other times not very subtle at all. More often than we would like to realize, our bars are self-imposed; they result from our insecurities and lack of love. I chose to demolish my bars and break through to freedom. Once I learned to do that, I began to live my dream.

CHAPTER 1:
THE HURRICANE

The first home I remember was in Habana, Cuba. It was a typical Caribbean-style house – two stories of grey concrete, with an almost-flat roof of red barrel tiles. The doors and the windows on the ground floor were covered with iron bars, but this did not seem strange to me, because most of the homes on the island also had bars. They were ornamental, quite pretty and often painted in colors to contrast with the rest of the home. We lived in a nice neighborhood, and the bars were meant to be decorative, but they were also quite practical – they were designed to deter robbers from breaking and entering just as much as they were meant to be decorative.

Our house had two entrances, one for the first floor, where my grandparents lived, and a second, independent door followed by a stairway that led to the second floor where I lived with my mother and father. Although there were two separate outside entrances to the home, we could also get downstairs to my grandparents' portion of the house by an inside stairway. We all lived together, rather than my parents and I living in an apartment above my grandparents. And living together was an emotional state, not just a physical one. I grew up very close to my grandmother and grandfather, mi abuela y abuelo, and I remember Abuela quite often being in charge of making decisions for the household.

One of my earliest memories remains vividly alive in my mind because of the many different feelings I experienced. It was 1954 or 1955, and I was about four or five years old. For me, the "hurricane" began several days before the wind began to blow or the first drops of rain hit the ground. The "storm" started with my family. There was shouting and yelling. I heard the neighbors discussing the hurricane that was coming our way. Inside our house the voices were raised as if danger and uncertainty were sure to come soon: "What should we do?" "How do we keep the windows from shattering?" "We need to board the windows!" "No, we won't be able to see what's happening if we board up." "Do we leave or do we stay?"

Everyone had a different opinion, and although I kept asking "what is going to happen?" no one seemed to be able to answer me – or maybe they did not want to answer me – and that scared me most of all. I feared for my father and grandfather who went to work every day and I also feared for my toys – if everyone was boxing their belongings, I thought, I should do the same with my toys! I saw my mother writing on the boxes, and since I did not know what to write I decided to mark my boxes with a circle and five lines – insisting it was a hand – I meant it to say "Don't touch. It's mine!" Eventually I realized I had a lot of toys.

The arguing and shouting went on for hours. I didn't understand much. I'd never heard the word hurricane before, and all I understood was that some kind of large storm was coming and that my family, particularly my mother, my grandmother and my Aunt Silvia, who had come to ride out the storm with us, were worried that our house would be blown away or that we would be flooded.

The house didn't really have a basement, but it was set on the high side of the street where we lived, and one had to drive downhill from the street to get into the garage, which was set under the house. This was the area they worried would flood, and rightly so since the drain in the middle of the garage floor seemed quite small for the amount of water I understood was expected to fall on us. They moved all of the boxes and suitcases and extra furniture out of the garage and up the stairs. The house grew even more crowded. Crowded with boxes, crowded with family members shouting at each other; it seemed as if when the first drops started to fall we were not yet prepared.

Lightly at first, the rain and the wind began. But as the storm became fiercer, I knew I had never heard anything like it. The wind howled and whistled, it seemed to be all around us; the rain pounded harder and harder. It was a constant barrage of noise that didn't let up – the noise from outside of the rain and the wind and the noise on the inside of the women of my family, worrying, praying and shouting at each other. I hoped that no one would notice me, and I tried to be inconspicuous, quietly looking out the large front window. I was worried. Although everyone had been in the house when the storm started, I had listened to them talking about what could happen – roofs blown away, windows shattered, houses washed away in floods. I worried quietly about myself and my family – would we survive?

Several times I heard large objects hit the house, the strong wind blowing a tree branch, a street sign, a garbage can, into and past the house. The house was taking too many hits; I was glad that whoever had been against boarding the windows had won that argument because I now had a great view of something I had never seen before. But I was also very scared because everyone in the house seemed petrified about what could happen next. I had never seen a storm like this before. I could hear the water rushing into the garage below the house.

The rain had become a river rushing down our road. The wind continued to blow leaves and tree limbs, even small trees and bushes past our window. I saw parts of other homes go flying or floating by. I was terrified. What was happening to the outside of my house? Was it being ripped into pieces?

Finally, Abuelo, who had mostly stayed quiet and calm throughout the previous days' discussion and arguments, noticed me. He seemed to understand that what worried me the most was the fear that the water would rise up from the basement and drown us all.

"Don't take him down there. He can't swim," my grandmother told my grandfather as we headed down the stairs. That just heightened my fear.

But when we got to the bottom of the steps, I understood why my grandfather had brought me there. Except for the sound of the water, it was quieter here. I couldn't hear the moaning of the wind or the shouting of the women. The noise was reduced to only the pounding of the rain on the wooden garage door.

The water had come into the now-empty garage, but it was only about a foot and a half; a little below the waist for a rather small five-year-old. The water looked clean, and even though it was swirling around the garage drain, it did not look as threatening in reality as the pictures that my mind had formed. I knew it was too shallow for me to drown. I knew it would never rise up those stairs and come into my house, and I immediately began to feel better.

"Let's make a fleet," Abuelo said.

He had brought paper and scissors and began to cut and make ships out of the paper. Large ones, small ones, about 15 in all; and he gave them to me to float around our garage. This was the turning point for me – my grandfather didn't talk to me much, he just showed me by his demeanor and by example that everything would be all right. I came out of this storm glad and happy to see the sun again and curious to see the downed trees and to hear about what other people experienced.

***

Never have I awakened saying, "I have figured it all out!" With me, it is always a step by step learning process. One day I realize one thing and three years from now something else hits me. The same is true with this memory of the hurricane.

Looking back, I wasn't catered to or babied. I was just considered another person by the rest of my family. For whatever reason, which no one has ever explained, I was just left to experience the hurricane as it went along. No one told me what to expect. Interestingly, given today's culture of getting down with our children and talking to them in order to explain situations, the attitude of my parents and grandparents was "just deal with it." Only my grandfather, who without saying anything except, "Come with me" and "Let's build a fleet," explained so very much. Interesting how such calm and detached behavior in contrast to the women and my father allowed me to understand, years later, so many valuable lessons.

After it was over the hurricane didn't seem as bad

as it had sounded and as it had felt. The worst part was hearing the people argue. And when it was over, I was curious to see what had happened to the world outside. It was devastation. But not to the extent I had anticipated. The house wasn't torn apart. I wasn't blown away. I didn't drown. I expected others to have blown away, and that hadn't happened, either.

Although I didn't realize at the time, I was, in fact learning, and I would eventually learn many things from this hurricane. I learned that I wanted to be closer to my grandfather. He had been the most right in his attitude toward the storm. "Let's play. It will be okay." He showed me the importance of remaining calm when dealing with bad news. This was the lesson I learned from the storm. Because of my grandfather's example, today when someone says that something is terrible, I know that it is time to calm things down and not rush to an emotional reaction.

I have also realized that in order to most effectively internalize a lesson we need to experience the situation. In dealing with my children, I have not tried to insulate them from the negative aspects of life. Life is a balance of positive and negative, and only by experiencing both do we realize how best to sustain that balance. Of course, I am not advocating survival training for a five-year-old during a hurricane. If, in the middle of the hurricane, my parents had kicked me out into the hurricane yelling, "Survive and don't come back until it's over!" I would have needed strong therapy – to say the least – if I had, in fact, managed to survive. However, I am also convinced that had my parents realized how they were ignoring me, they might have acted differently. But life is a balance, and if they had not ignored me before and during the storm, I would not have learned the lessons I did. So, it seems to me that even when we behave in a manner that may not be the best or most appropriate at the time, positive things can still result.

***

Soon after the hurricane, my family made plans to move to what I remember as an interim apartment or small house. I was upset because I did not know why they were moving, and I had friends and loved my old home. Would I make friends at the new house? And just as with the hurricane, no one explained. I was about six years old then, and I was getting pretty tired of not being told things. I didn't like the feeling of just being told what to do. It wasn't until just before we moved that I found out why we were moving.

Prior to learning about the move, my family argued a lot. What was all the yelling about? I wondered, and said to myself, "Here we go again." Once again I anticipated disaster. Once again there were packing and worries, this time about the new neighborhood. I was told I wouldn't be able to go outside to play, and this made me fearful about what would happen to me – why couldn't I go out and play? I think this second experience of chaos, following only a short time after the hurricane, is why I began my rebellious years at a very early age. My family had been fanatical about that hurricane, but it was not as life threatening as they said it would be. Now they were making a big deal about something again, and at six years old I had already learned that my family could really exaggerate a situation. I began to rely on my grandfather and his judgment more than that of the rest of the family. Once again he was quiet while the rest of the family was in an uproar.

But there was another aspect of the move that worried me. My grandfather and grandmother were not coming with us to the new house, and I didn't know why! I was going to miss my grandfather, and also I really trusted him. Finally he explained to me that he and my parents were in the process of building another house; one where they would again live downstairs and my mother and father and I would live upstairs. We had to move to this small home first though, because it would take about a year for the new house to be completed.

The house my family lived in during the hurricane. You can see the garage. My father is standing in front of the house.

We did move, and my life in that temporary neighborhood was not a happy one. My parents always seemed to worry about being robbed; I was not allowed to make friends without them being cleared by my parents. Life was boring, I had no friends. I remember a long hallway where the housing units were set out in a row; we had a neighbor to our right and a neighbor to our left. I don't remember going to school then and I was lonely and there wasn't much I could do. Fortunately, we were not there long and soon moved to our new house as my grandfather had explained. I was so glad to have him once again living with us, exactly as he had said; my parents and I upstairs and my grandparents downstairs.

That year I started school at a Catholic school, the Marist Brothers in Habana. We were now living in a suburb of Habana called La Vibora, on a street called Calle Nueva. As it turned out this was the perfect place for me to live, given the things that would take place in my life during the next four or so years. From one perspective, it was a quiet street with lots of children on the block and more moving in every day. At its height, we numbered 12 children ranging in age from eight to 12 years of age, and we all played together. Most owned bikes, and we thought we had a perfect neighborhood. On our individual birthdays the kids planned the parties; our parents just paid for them and implemented what we decided. For example, when I turned nine years old, we wanted a rock and roll party featuring music from Elvis Presley and others. Another night my father took five of us, the oldest boys, to the city of Habana to see the new release of the movie, *The Time Machine*. To an extrovert like me, this was heaven.

However, life is not perfect. I remember a day soon after we moved in. It was during my first year at the Marist school, and I was seven years old. My father came to pick me up. I was called into the principal's office, and in front of the Brother Principal he told me that he and my mother had gotten divorced. At first, I had no idea what that meant. I knew that my parents constantly fought and that my grandmother used to also fight a lot with my mother. My mother owned a beauty salon; eventually she owned two salons. She was a hair dresser and a business woman during the 1950s in Cuba where the culture dictated that the married woman would remain in the home bringing up the children. My mother, in many ways, was ahead of her times, and years later I realized that one has to be careful not to blindly accept existing cultural norms or be afraid to approach situations from different perspectives. However, on that day, as I learned of my parents' divorce while standing in front of the school principal, I wasn't thinking about things like this. I wondered, "Why tell me here? Why not at home?" Divorce was not acceptable in society at that time, particularly not in the Catholic culture of Cuba. I did not know any children of divorced parents. The only thing that I understood was that when I returned home that day my mother would not be there.

I was devastated. I felt sick; I started to sweat, and I wanted to throw up. I was so very sad and angry that I wanted to cry, but I held it back. What had I done wrong? Immediately all the times I'd gotten into trouble came to mind, and I started to blame myself. I wanted to do it over again. I would do things differently; I would behave better. This could not happen, it had to be corrected. Why couldn't we think this over? Years later I realized I should have let it all out to show how much hurt I felt. I thought about all the arguments I had witnessed, everyone criticizing my mother, saying that she was acting in a way she should not, and she wasn't there at the school that day. I heard from the principal that she was abandoning me. I remembered hearing my mother tell my father that he should not listen to his mother; that his mother was meddling in their lives. Who was right, and who was wrong?

I was an only child; I did not have a brother or sister with whom to talk about this. I could not talk about it with friends. I did not know anyone whose parents were divorced, and I was embarrassed to talk about it. One thing I knew at that moment – my grandmother was the boss of the family. My father never, ever, went against her.

***

Two years later, January 1, 1959, was an historic day that eventually affected me personally, although at age nine I did not understand how significant it was. That was the date that the revolution led by Fidel Castro succeeded. Fulgencio Batista, the then dictator in Cuba, was forced to leave the country, and Castro led a triumphant takeover of La Habana, the capital of Cuba.

Everyone seemed overjoyed, everyone seemed ready for freedom to eradicate the inhumane treatment and killings that had marked Batista's regime. Castro wore rosary beads on his neck and promised freedom and liberty. My family shared these hopes and aspirations. However, a few weeks into the new government, my father began to express caution about what was being said and done by revolution leaders. One day, over my grandmother's objections, my father told me to get into his car; that he was going to teach me that actions are more important than words. My father and I drove into Habana city proper, and what I saw chilled me.

People, unrestrained by Castro's soldiers standing by, were looting furniture from homes, burning them at times. People were being beaten by gangs, and I saw several knifings where the people were left on the street to bleed. There was silence in the car. The only thing I remember my father saying was, "The revolution was fought to bring justice and freedom and stop senseless killing – that is what was said. You look at the actions with soldiers standing by – do the deeds match the words? Deeds are more important than words."

As I returned home I felt older. I had just seen blood in the streets and learned that the personal experiences that I had felt were so terrible – my parents' divorce, for example – were not as important as losing one's life, or the life of a loved one. Even in times of joy bad things happen – life is not perfect. Or is it? What is perfect? Is life what we make of it, how we act and react as opposed to what happens to us?

To this day, I go back to that time as the first time I realized that our actions do not always match our words. Unknown to my father at the time, I kept thinking, "You always tell me you love me but your behavior just before and during the divorce did not match what you told me."

I had the opportunity before he died to confront

him about why he let his mother break up his marriage, but he never gave me an answer. Sometimes we just don't get closure in life, and we must just move on. The change in my home life after the divorce, the fights between my parents and the way in which my grandmother acted toward my mother were some of the reasons why two years later, at 11 years old, I welcomed the decision to send me out of Cuba, alone, to the United States. Leaving Cuba wasn't as traumatic for me as it would have been for someone with a happy home life. Years later I realized that I began to grow up emotionally at age seven, the day I learned about my parents' divorce.

We learn more from the bad or negative experiences in our lives than from the good. Positive things can result from bad situations, and negative things can result from good situations. I learned at an early age that I had a lot of control in my life, more than I realized at first. I was outgoing, I had friends, and I had good times with them. I had a lot of control over my social life. I had many cousins on my mother's side; she was the youngest of eight brothers and sisters, so when I was with her I always had cousins to play with. I enjoyed wonderful times with each parent, individually. But every time the family got together they pulled against the other. I was asked who I loved more. Eventually, I got fed up and lashed out.

"I don't want to hear that from you anymore!" I loved them both, and I told my parents I wanted those questions to stop. The first time this happened was after my father had taken me on our driving experience through rebellion-torn Habana. For the first time I stood up for myself – I was about nine at that time. I had learned that if I stood my ground I could favorably affect the quality of my life.

Chapter 2:
Out of Cuba

After we moved to the new house every day seemed to bring something new into our lives. My relationship with my grandfather continued to grow. We often just played catch together, and I wanted to hear stories about him; I was particularly interested in his life as a teenager. His parents had sent him to study in the United States, in Pennsylvania, and I was impressed by the fact that he spoke perfect English. I realized there was a lot more I wanted to learn about him, and I enjoyed, very much, my time with him.

The only other stable part of my life revolved around my many friends on our block. As children, we lived in a world of our own, playing our games – Cowboys and Indians, soccer, baseball, emulating the heroes of the Cuban revolution, arranging each others' birthday parties, riding and racing our bicycles around our neighborhood, talking about school and all in all growing ever closer to each other. As far as we were concerned, except for Christmas holidays, nothing going on around us mattered much.

Prior to 1961, Christmas was celebrated throughout Cuba, and in La Habana, particularly, in a big and pretentious fashion. People decorated their homes with such spectacular displays of nativity scenes and bright lights that entire neighborhoods were lit up with happiness and joy. My friends and I enjoyed walking along with great numbers of people; we were just horsing around and viewing the decorated homes and speaking with the homeowners about their decorations. In 1959 and 1960 there were competitions for

My paternal grandparents,
Santiago and Manuela Paz

the best decorated homes, and my friends and I held our own contests by betting on the results. We always looked forward to these times with great anticipation. Christmas season was long in Cuba; January 6, Dia de los Reyes Magos or Three Kings Day, was even more important than Christmas Day. Yes, Santa Claus would drop by with toys on Christmas Day, but we also took great pleasure in having another crack at figuring out how our presents could appear overnight on January 6, because more gifts for the children were left on Three Kings Day than on Christmas Day. As we grew older, we did not want to admit who really gave us our gifts for fear that they would stop coming. And they did. The presents stopped on Christmas of 1961.

***

On April 17, 1961, Cuban exile groups totaling approximately 1,400 men supported by the CIA invaded Cuba at the Bay of Pigs on the southern coast of the island in an unsuccessful attempt to overthrow the Castro government. President Dwight D. Eisenhower had first approved the operation, although by the time it was carried out President John F. Kennedy was in power. The invasion was intended to create the spark for uprisings within Cuba, but within days of the invasion the Cuban government had successfully secured the invasion zone or Playa Giron at the mouth of the Bay, and had killed or captured most of the invaders. Because after the Bay of Pigs Castro asked the Soviet Union to install nuclear weapons in Cuba for defense against the United States, this unsuccessful attempt to overthrow Castro would later spark the 13-day missile crisis in October 1962, which brought the United States to the brink of nuclear war with the Soviet Union.

I was ten years old at the time, and early that morning I sensed something was wrong. Neighbors were visiting each other before breakfast, and I do not remember going to school that day. There seemed to be a lot of secrecy among the adults. Something was happening that they did not deem they needed to inform us, the children. Word started to reach my family from neighbors that Cuba had just been invaded by the United States. My grandmother was agitated and scared as she attempted to contact my father at his work and could not reach him. I, too, grew scared as night fell and no one was able to tell me where my father was or what had happened to him. I imagined that he had been sent to fight the invasion and realized he was neither a soldier nor knew how to shoot. I was afraid he would never come home, that he had been killed. For the next several days I grew more convinced that my father had died, and I cried often. Later, from neighbors, we learned that the chances were that he had been detained because similar experiences were taking place in several places throughout the island and thousands had been arrested by the Castro government to prevent a potential uprising of the people in sympathy with the invaders. But nothing was known for sure, and I was confused and felt so alone – what had happened to my father? Or what would happen to him? News came to us in pieces, and no matter how much information we received, I seemed to always have more questions than answers. They all revolved around what had happened to my father, but no one was interested in talking to me. Since my mother no longer lived with us, I could not communicate with her either, and also I did not know where she was or what had happened to her. The Castro government was saying that Cuba had been invaded by the United States, accompanied by Cuban exiled troops; that battles were raging, and we were at war. Cuba was under attack, and Fidel Castro was personally taking command of the Cuban defenses. The fighting was fierce, and many had died. Defeat American imperialism, was the cry, "Patria o Muerte" – "Homeland or Death."

My father had never been involved in politics, and it scared me to think that the government was making a mistake and he would be killed. Three days passed without any word of his whereabouts – no one knew where my father was; I could not eat or sleep, and it seemed as if each day things got worse.

Then the news – the invasion force had been thoroughly defeated, there were many deaths, many taken prisoner and Castro was emboldened and raging.

He gave speeches saying all who were against the freedom of Cuba and the Revolution would be killed. Schools were shut down, and we had no clue as to where my father was. Rumors were circulating that the militia forces had taken people prisoner and were killing those who were found to be against the Revolution. I agonized – was my father among them? What would happen to me and my family if my father had been killed? I felt completely inadequate; there was nothing I could do. Abuela continued doing what she seemed to find very effective: crying out for mercy to all the saints. She was just out of control, so I sought out Abuelo.

"¿Esta tu hijo muerto?" "Is your son dead?" That's how I put it.

"Todo se arregla." "All will work out."

At the time I felt that did not help me; although I felt calmer I still had no answers. But in his way, Abuelo was telling me that there was nothing we could do at the moment. He did not know whether his son would ever return home alive, but at that moment there was nothing he could do to control his son's fate. All he could do was wait; whatever happened life would go on.

In the years since, I have revisited this experience many times, and I have come to realize that it is not what happens to us that we should fear, but how we handle it after it occurs. What we do today brings consequences in the future, and although we generally cannot control what others do, we can consider the possible consequences or reactions before we act so we can better understand what others may do. In any event, we need to go on, we need to persevere and be strong in facing what has happened. My grandfather seemed to know just how much he should and could say to me.

Finally on the fourth day, my father just walked into our house – my heart jumped! I felt so happy. He was unshaven, disheveled, weak, filled with disgust for the things he had seen. I had never seen him like this but still, he looked just wonderful to me. He and I strongly hugged each other, and I did not want to let go. He did not say much to anyone about anything; all he would say in my presence was, "I was not allowed to come home."

One thing I failed to realize then, but looking back I now understand, is that my family's life completely and irrevocably changed the day my father came home. He was a different man, driven to a purpose, which at the time I did not know. The fact was that life for all my friends would also change in ways none of us could have anticipated before April 17, 1961.

The events that transpired after that date were dramatic and horrifying to me. I had never imagined that individuals could act in the ways that I saw in the next few months. The Catholic school I attended was taken over by the government militia. I was in class when the soldiers entered the school. Soldiers were posted at all doors leading out of the school, soldiers patrolled the surrounding streets, and another group of soldiers entered the chapel and broke into the sanctuary and started to remove all religious signs and statues, throwing the chalice with the Holy Eucharist on the ground. I think that was the most frightening thing of all. Who were these people? In Cuba just about everyone was Catholic and understood what a grave mortal sin defiling the body of Jesus was, and yet these soldiers were doing it! If they could do this to Jesus, what could they do to me and my friends? We were nothing to them! I have never felt more scared and vulnerable than I did that day.

After this incident, a new school opened there, and later the building continued to be a place of fear and injustice by serving as a jail. But in 1961, my father took me out of that school, and I did not return to any school for another 10 months, when I left Cuba and arrived in the United States.

One by one, all my friends were leaving Cuba. During the next three months, four of my friends on the block left the country, including a beautiful girl on whom I had a wonderful crush. She, with her older sister, younger brother and her parents, went to Puerto Rico. Her father was a pharmacist. I have never seen any of them again. Christmas 1961 did not exist; it was done. Castro had declared he was a Marxist Communist and Cuba would be a Marxist Communist country. The only thing that my family explained to me was that a Marxist Communist does not believe in God, and as I thought about that I wondered how someone who had worn rosary beads on his day of triumph could now say neither he nor his country would believe in God – how could someone first believe in God and suddenly denounce Him? How could someone just order everyone in an entire country to stop believing in God? How could that happen? Regardless, I came face to face with how Castro could control others: just tell them you own them, have your troops march into schools and change them. These were actions that had been unimaginable a few months before, but suddenly people just executed such orders. Castro said he wanted freedom and yet he allowed and encouraged violence against those who did not agree with him.

I was starting to connect some dots – 1959, the looting and violence my father showed me; 1961, the takeover of my school, the arrest or detainment of people without reason. I did not feel good about where I was. On top of that, I continued to deal with the aftermath of my parents' divorce, with constant battles regarding visitation rights with my mother, since my father had retained parental custody. I was also trying to understand the one-by-one loss of my friends as they, with their parents, fled Cuba.

Also during this time, a new development that had started a year earlier gained prominence and influence in our lives – the Defense Committee was established by the Castro government to keep an eye on the "safety" of our neighborhood, and it would maintain vigilance over the movement of the people in the neighborhood. The house to our right became such a place – two sisters, spinsters, who pretty much lived in seclusion, suddenly became the most powerful people on our block. Any house where people gathered, the sisters had to be informed of the purpose and identification of those attending. No one could take in a relative without first obtaining approval from the local Defense Committee staff. Our neighborhood and block had changed; my birthday in July, when I turned 11 years old, was much different than in prior years. My friends had dwindled from 12 to seven, and we spent much of our time talking about those who were gone and thinking about what would happen to each of us. Our parents had already warned us not to say anything bad about the government, and I had a lot of anger and trouble about that – I wanted to say what I wanted and did not like to be silenced – bad times for extroverts!

By December 1961, there were five of us left, and when I left two months later in February, 1962, only three friends were still in the neighborhood. During my last several months in Cuba I felt increasingly less and less in control of my surroundings. We were no longer planning and enjoying our birthday parties. Our parents would not discuss anything with us for fear we would tell each other and somehow their plans would come to the attention of our Defense Committee. Everyone lived in fear, and we began to hear that the Castro government was rounding up children our age to take them to camps where they would be indoctrinated into the Marxist principles or shipped to the Soviet Union for further education – that meant we would be separated from our parents, and the Revolution, not our parents, would be responsible for our upbringing.

In January, swearing me to secrecy, my mom and dad began talking to me about leaving Cuba ,and at first I thought that like my friends who had previously left with their parents for Spain or Puerto Rico, that I would leave with both my mom and dad. Although they had said nothing about my grandparents and I did not know whether my grandfather would also be leaving, for once in a very long time my mom and dad were in complete agreement. Not only were they not fighting, they seemed friendly towards each other – divorce in reverse, I thought, and I was all for it!

"When are we leaving?" I asked. Their response deflated me and scared me at the same time. My parents' plan was to send me out of the country alone, without them, by way of our church, and as they would often repeat, "We don't know when we can join you in the United States, but we will do everything we can to do so as soon as we can."

In fact, during this time, my father applied to leave the country and was fired from his job. My mother, since she had a business, faced an even more difficult path to leaving. They both told me there was no way, even if they would never see me again, that they would continue to expose me, to risk my future in a Communist country run by evil people where I would never enjoy the benefits of freedom and opportunity to live my life the way I chose, to the best of my abilities. My mother often told me to follow her footsteps and do what I thought correct, not necessarily what society expected of me. I paid attention to her because she had shown that to me by being a young business woman in Cuba in the 1950s and early 1960s.

So, my parents' "brilliant" idea to spare me from the grasp of Castro's government was to fly me out of Cuba by myself to Miami, Florida, where people unknown to them would pick me up and take me to a camp with other children approximately my age and perhaps never see me again! At first this sounded so desperate to me, and scary. I was completely without any control of anything, and my future was being decided for me by others. While two of those people were my parents, who I knew loved me very much, there were suddenly others involved in my life who didn't even know me. I did not know it at the time but I would have about six weeks to take all of this in before my departure, and to my surprise I would have an amazing reversal of expectations from the day in December when my parents first told me I would leave the country alone until February 6, 1962, when I left the country, never to see it again until September 2009, 47 years later.

Operation Pedro Pan, as it became known, took place from 1960 to 1962 and was coordinated by the U.S. Department of State, and some say that Castro spread the word that the CIA was also involved and the Catholic Archdiocese of Miami. It involved placing approximately 14,000 children who were sent away from Cuba without their parents into the hands of the church and placing them in foster homes all over the United States; some with relatives or friends, others in group homes in about 35 states.

I am not exactly sure when my mental approach changed regarding going to the United States, but I remember very vividly that for me, my departure day started the day before, on the night of February 5. I had struggled with how badly I felt each time one of my friends had left without saying goodbye, so I was determined not to have my remaining friends feel that way. I betrayed my father's instructions not to tell anyone, and on that night I told them. I did not understand why I could not mention it to my friends, since everyone knew that my father had filed his papers to leave Cuba and had consequently been fired from his job. He had been labeled a "gusano" or "worm" because he was giving up on the Revolution. Already the girl I had a crush on, Argelia Garcia, had left without my telling her how I had felt about her, and I was now leaving the two brothers I was closest to, Alberto and Armando. So, I told my remaining friends that I was leaving, and we said our good-byes. We shed tears together, recalling all the good times we had and promising we would never fight against each other if the United States had to fight Cuba. Although we did not discuss the possibility of never seeing each other again, I knew that since some of their parents were for the Revolution, we probably would never see each other again, and we never have met.

That night I also sought out my grandfather, and I spent a significant amount of time with him. We played catch in the central hallway of my house, and as I heard my grandmother crying at times, he smiled and complimented me on how well I had learned to play sports and told me that I should continue to play and always improve. He told me that he knew the United States and I would like it very much. He said that he and my grandmother planned to follow us to the United States and we would be together again someday. He expected to see me do very well there; he was not sad, he was happy for me. He mentioned that no matter what happened everything would work out for the best – "todo va a estar bien." "It will be okay", he said in Spanish. He told me to just do my best and never give up. "Be yourself," he said, in everything, just like in sports. He explained to me what a great sacrifice my mom and dad were making in letting me go like this. This was the first time I had spoken with my grandfather in quite a while, but he made me feel important and that I had to do well always.

My father put me to bed that night, and all seemed

quiet. So much had happened since those early days in 1959, less than two years before, when he drove me through the streets of La Habana to show me the violence condoned by the Revolution, until he and my mother told me in December 1961 that I was going to leave the country. I did not completely understand why all this had happened, but this was the first time since those days in 1959 that he and I spoke father-to-son. I have never forgotten his words and how I felt.

"Your mother and I love you very much, and it is because we love you that we will risk never seeing you again," he told me. "We have both begun to file papers to follow you to the United States. We want to be with you, but if we are not able to join you, I want you to know it is not because we have not tried; it will not be our fault, but the fault of the Cuban government."

He told me that good people would be responsible for feeding me and providing me with a home, and I would be taken care of. He explained to me the program, which became known as the "Pedro Pan flights," and said I would not be alone; other boys and girls would be there with me.

"We want you to go to the United States because neither of us wants you to ever be forced to become a Communist. We want you to have the freedom to do what you think best with your life, and we want you to have the freedom to believe in God.

"As you grow up we want you to always be honest and always do good towards others. Never give up hope; you are now in control of what you do – don't do stupid things."

I asked many questions – What would happen to them when I left? Would he and my mother be arrested? When would Abuelo and Abuela follow? I asked him if I did anything wrong in the United States would he find out? He said "yes" to this, and smiled. I also asked where

I would stay in the United States and he explained that I would go to Florida where I would stay for a while before they placed me in another state, like New Jersey where my Uncle Higinio, my mother's brother, lived. He kissed me on my forehead and said he would wake me up soon because the plane was leaving early in the morning and we would meet my mother at the airport. I was already packed with a small bag, a carry-on, which was the only luggage I was allowed to take with me; no jewelry or watches, just a small amount of clothing. As my father left my room I felt happy and excited; I was going on an adventure that would determine what kind of person I would become. I knew what my parents expected of me.

***

Given the environment that had become my day-to-day life, going to the United States seemed the key to my future. I went to bed feeling ready and important. Something was happening to me, and even though I did not totally understand it, I did like the idea. In effect, at 11 years old, my father gave me control of much of my life. Without threatening me with punishment, he empowered me to trust in my own instincts and live my life. As parents today, what would it take for us to do that? When and how do we begin to empower our children to be responsible for themselves? When do we overprotect or shelter our children from life? How much responsibility do we give our children?

I have learned that in facilitating the growth of my children the answers to these questions revolve around creating a balance between the existing circumstances, the environment and the individual child. I realize today that at age 11 I had a lot more control than I realized. Most of that control lay in what I could do in response to the events taking place around me. I definitely compromised my desires by not objecting to my parents' wishes, maybe because their actions were sufficiently explained to me and I knew that I had my family's complete support and trust.

Breakfast on the morning of February 6 was nearly an impossibility. I sat in my home, attempting to eat as usual when I had no idea how this day would end. The next memory I have is of my mother sitting with me at the airport until the time came when I was asked to leave my parents, pass through into a room to be searched and walk to the boarding station. My heart was racing. Except for my parents, everything and everyone seemed to be out of control. There were five or six of us children boarding the plane, and they and their parents all seemed to be crying or yelling or cursing. The people processing us did not speak to us in a friendly tone. They treated everyone who was leaving with disrespect.

By contrast, my parents were calm, and they did not show me tears. Through a glass partition we waved goodbye and threw kisses – I saw their smiles – how strong they were! They were with me; they thought I could do this, and in doing so they gave me confidence that I could. Although it may seem heretical, I found myself looking forward to boarding that plane to Miami and my next phase in life. This was the first time I had been in an airplane, and as the twin engines roared to life and the plane took off, I saw for the first time my homeland, my birthplace, from high above and realized that I might never return. I said a silent goodbye, and looked to the front of the plane.

Chapter 3:
Finding My Voice

Sitting by the window in the plane on m first flight was a "trip!" The furthest things from my mind were the changes that would take place in my life and the lessons I would learn in the coming months. For the moment I just sat there, looking out the window. There was nothing but water underneath, and it hit me – I am all alone, there is no turning back. Who will meet me? I was wearing a tag that identified me, but what if something went wrong? What if I wasn't on the list when I arrived in Miami? What would happen to me?

These thoughts conflicted with the sense of adventure I had talked about with the friends I had left behind. I had heard so much about Miami and the United States, and I was headed there. I felt important that so much was being done for me. So many people had gone out of their way for me, and we didn't even know each other. I could understand doing good things for my friends and respecting our elders and parents, all this had been taught to us in Cuba before my parents pulled me out of school. But strangers helping each other...in religion class I had heard about loving your neighbor, now it was starting to become a bit clearer to me. Lots of strangers had, and were about to, help me for quite some time to come. This reassured me, and I felt calm. Although I didn't understand it at the time, this was the moment that became the foundation, throughout my adult life, for volunteering to improve the quality of life of others. I now realize that one life experience conveys many lessons, and it is in our best interest to pay attention to them; looking back at these experiences helps tremendously to focus on these lessons.

As we landed, I realized that I had really enjoyed the takeoff and landing and wanted to do it again, but most of my memories of that day, in fact of the next few months, are like snapshots: clear, still photos of a moment in time, an impression of feelings or thoughts. Click: the snapshot is taken, the picture is a crystal clear image of that moment, but the surrounding minutes, hours, even days around it are gone.

I looked around and saw a brother and sister around my age. The boy, who was younger, was crying, and his sister was trying to calm him down while appearing upset herself. This was not easy for anyone of us who left our homes in this way. I don't remember leaving the plane; my next memory is entering the terminal where a couple looked at my tag and told me to go with them. I followed as instructed. I don't remember the type of vehicle I entered, but with me were the brother and sister I had seen at the plane. We drove for what seemed a long distance and arrived at what I later learned was a camp somewhere in south central Florida. Several camps had been set up throughout South Florida to temporarily house us until we were redeployed elsewhere within the

United States. The children who were under 13 years old were separated into boys and girls dormitories, and children 13 or older were located in another camp in Kendal, Florida. Things moved so fast that day I arrived; I remember nothing else except that I was given a bunk bed in a room where four of us slept.

On the first day there I met the rest of the boys staying at that residence. I think that there were about eight of us, although my memory of that time is blurry. I remember there was a building that may have been a duplex where we stayed. I remember being given a tour of the camp and shown where we would eat, where the

My parents, Marta Paz y Bravo and Santiago (Macho) Martinez y Martinez

chapel, the infirmary and the classrooms were. We were kept busy from Mondays through Fridays with English and math classes. I welcomed English lessons since I did not know a word of the language. Math classes were very easy for me.

As I sat in that class I remembered that in Cuba, at the Marist Brothers school, the Brothers gave us weekly report cards that ranked us in order and on Fridays we were tested, in writing and verbally. We had to stand up in class and calculate the numbers they gave us in the time allotted for our response. I also thought about my father getting furious if I placed lower than third in the class of about 30 students – this occurred once and I was grounded for a week. I was pushed at an early age to do my very best and to be the very best – that pressure made these classes feel like a breeze, but I just could never concentrate on them; too many things were occupying space in my head, mainly dealing with increasing isolation and the events I felt I could not control throughout my stay in that camp.

My second day I wrote my first letter to my mother and father and gave them the address where to write me. I missed them very much already, and this was just my second sunrise in the United States. Even though I had always been very outgoing and friendly I didn't want to reach out to other boys or girls in the camp. I felt empty about first seeing my friends leave in Cuba and then leaving other good friends behind, knowing I would probably never see them again. I had been told I would not be in this camp too long, and I did not want to make good friends again, only to be separated and never hear from them again.

I remembered my grandfather and I had played sports: baseball, softball and basketball. In the camp we had teams and played competitively. I enjoyed that so much that I always looked forward to the next games. Once again my grandfather was right; I made sports a part of my life. Because I did not want to make good friends, I made acquaintances and became very quiet and wanted to be alone, but at the same time I struggled with the outgoing side of my nature. I wanted friends, and it took a lot for me not to seek out the others in the camp. When I had been there about a week I spotted a very beautiful girl who seemed so happy, and I wanted very much to be friends with her and ask why she was so happy. I never approached her though, because I remembered Argelia back in Cuba and how abandoned I felt when one morning she was no longer there. I did not want to feel like that again, and as if I had prophesized it, one day I looked for this girl and she was gone. I asked her friend where she was, and learned she had been sent to another state. The friend told me, "You know, she liked you but she thought you did not like her because you never talked to her." As if I could have felt any worse! I felt a sinking feeling in my stomach, I was so confused! What if?

I am not certain why my memories of my time in the camp are so spotty. However, I do recollect certain events that happened within the five-month period that I lived there. My grandmother had given me the phone number of a cousin of hers who lived with her husband and her sister in Coral Gables, Florida. My grandmother told me to call her and she might be able to pick me up on some weekends so that I could call my dad in Cuba. I made contact with them, and we arranged for them to pick me up the second weekend I was there. I did remember seeing them in Cuba; they were wonderful and always treated me with love and attention. They were older than my grandmother, and two of them were ill, and one would soon pass away. The other was dealing with a disabled son, so they were not a consistent refuge to me, and even if they could have been, I was not thrilled with spending my weekends with much older people. But being with them offered me the opportunity to talk on the telephone to my dad; the first time I had spoken with him in the two weeks since I had arrived. He told me that his paperwork was moving along well and he expected to leave Cuba in March, only six weeks or so after I had left. This made me very happy, and I was told by my relatives that they would pick me up again in mid-March. I was looking forward so much to that weekend because I was certain I would hear from my dad at that time that he was on his way to me.

Of course, things do not always go the way we want them to go, and a few days before my next visit with my cousins I fell very ill with a high fever. I was sent to the infirmary and placed on a cot along with several other boys – we all had come down with chicken pox. I had never heard of chicken pox, and I kept insisting that it could not possibly be chicken pox because I had not been anywhere near any chickens! I thought I must have something else and they did not want to tell me; I was weak, feverish and I cried out to a nurse "I want my mommy!" I was afraid I would die.

Since I was still sick the weekend I was supposed to be picked up by my relatives, I could not go with them. Distant cousins called the camp, and a nurse told me that my mom and dad knew I had the chicken pox and also that my dad would not be coming in March as he had thought. Again, I thought, things could not get any worse. There was nothing I could do; I could not control anything, and I felt angry and fearful – what would happen to me? There was nothing else I could do to help my father get to the United States, so I asked a nurse to tell me all about chicken pox and what else I could get sick with. My fears included wondering what other strange diseases I could get in this country – I needed lots more information. Of course the nurse, who was very good to me, said she really could not say how many other diseases I could get sick with, so I told her to bring me someone who could – that didn't happen so I started writing letters to my mom and dad telling them I thought they had made a mistake and that I could die here. I can only imagine the hurt I caused them when they received that letter, but they never mentioned it to me. I know I was not a very good patient and caused my parents a lot of anxiety.

When I was finally released from the infirmary I called my relatives, telling them I was fine and I wanted to talk to my dad and asked when they could pick me up. They never did, but the couple who watched over us in our residence told me they had left a message for me that my dad would be arriving in the United States on April 27, 1962. I also received word from the camp leaders that the next week, late in April but before my father was scheduled to arrive, that I would be transferred to New Mexico.

Could no one here do anything right? Not even the adults had gotten this right; my awe for authority was dashed. I felt isolated, angry, completely ignored and scared I was about to miss the only opportunity to see my parents again. I had to stop this move to New Mexico, and the only way to do so was to speak up and hold my ground. Out of nowhere I felt a strange sense of confidence and purpose. At the age of 11, when I could think of nothing else to stop all of these things that were happening to me, I found I had a voice and asked to speak to whoever was in charge. I insisted so much that I finally was allowed to speak to a man who told me he was in charge of the transfers.

"My parents did not send me here to the United States so you could send me off to another country," I told him angrily, in Spanish.

The man laughed. "New Mexico is in the United States."

"I don't care if I am going to Old or New Mexico; I am staying in the United States! I have an uncle in New Jersey. It is to New Jersey that I want to go, not to Mexico, por favor!"

I made sure I added that "por favor." Although I was at the end of my rope and was now out of control, my parents told me always to be respectful, and I thought that after throwing a tantrum I should say "please." The man looked at me and told me that he would see what he could do.

I did not go to New Mexico. At the end of April I was in Florida hugging my dad for the first time in many weeks, and on June 6, 1962, four months after arriving in the United States, my father and I headed to New Jersey. I was going to the orphanage in Totowa and my father to Union City to start his life so that eventually I would be allowed to live with him again. No one knew how long that would take, but I had my own schedule for returning to my father, and I did not discuss it with anyone. I had been able to change New Mexico to New Jersey, and I had learned that I could influence some things. I planned to be living with my father by the end of that summer. At 11 years old I was starting to feel in control, and frankly, I liked that feeling. Today I wonder how I would have been impacted had the head of that camp in Florida denied my request and sent me to New Mexico – how fickle life can be!

Chapter 4:
An Adventure
Blindfolded

The day that my father and I flew from Miami to New Jersey was one more day in a long year filled with firsts. I was excited when I saw that the plane we would fly on was a jet – the plane which had flown me out of Cuba had been an older, twin engine model. But this excitement quickly passed, because along with this exciting "first," was a less pleasant "second." For the second time I had to leave my father.

Once we landed at Newark Airport, my dad was headed one way and I another. I was to be taken to an orphanage. As we said our goodbyes I asked him how I could contact him; he didn't know, but said he would contact me as soon as he could. That did not make me feel better – I wanted us to be a family again. I also did not fully understand how he would find me. I was no longer a trusting child. I asked him if he knew where I was going, and although he knew the name of the orphanage, he did not know where it was. We exited quickly out of the airport, and I was taken in a van and driven to Totowa, New Jersey. I have forgotten the name of the orphanage although St. Mary's rings a big bell.

The trip from Newark Airport to the orphanage took us through a mixture of older bridges and factories with smokestacks rising in a grayish and dark-looking panorama, which made me feel sad – is this the place I had insisted I be brought to? I asked myself this question, and it did nothing to lift my spirits. Once again, I did not know exactly when I would see my dad again. I did not say much during the trip but I kept wondering whether I had made a mistake by having us sent to New Jersey. The environment was not comparing favorably to the middle class neighborhood I had lived in La Vibora, Habana or the rural area in Florida where I had just spent several months. As we drove further away from the airport, however, I began to see a change in the scenery, and by the time we arrived at the orphanage I had noticed that I was now in a better area; there were more trees, nicer homes and more fields or wooded landscapes – I liked to draw, and the open spaces full of nature made me feel happier and less deflated.

At the orphanage, I met the Catholic nun who ran the home, and she seemed very nice and spoke to me in a soft and welcoming voice. She warned me that I would be sharing a large salon with other boys and I should be at my best behavior since there would be punishment for disobeying the instructions of the other sisters – fighting among the boys would not be tolerated and discipline would be immediately dispensed. I was also told that we would be called for meals and we should eat as quickly as possible and without any incidents. The

Mother Superior could not tell me how long I would be there; all she could say was that I could expect to remain for about a month. She explained that we were already into June and school was nearing an end, so I would not be expected to attend classes. All of this was told to me through an interpreter because although I had attended English classes in the Florida camp, I still did not speak a word of English.

Soon after lights out the first night one of the boys about my age, either in the third or fourth bed to my right, got into a fight with the fellow in the bed beside him, and they rolled on the ground, making lots of noise and yelling.

Almost as soon as the fight started, a rather large nun quickly stepped into the room, turned the lights on and moved swiftly to break up the fight. Without asking any questions she pivoted to her right and swung a left hook to the boy who had started the fight. He reared back, and without missing a step she wheeled again to her right and similarly administered a second left hook to the other boy. No further questions were asked; the two boys lay down to sleep and except for small sobs that I could hear, nothing more was done about the issue, that night or the next day. I had just experienced "immediate justice dispensed." Never again while I was there did I see those boys fight with each other or with anyone else. I fell asleep thinking about an incident when I was in kindergarten in Cuba at the Marist Brothers School.

***

I was about six years old and was punished for talking too much. My punishment, the Brother told me, was that the next day I would be sent to the dungeon in the school basement where many large rats lived. That entire day and night I agonized, but I did not tell my father about what was going to happen to me the next day. The following day on my way to the school bus, I saw our neighbor's cat and "borrowed" him without my neighbor's knowledge and snuck him in my school bag so he would help me fight the rats. When I got to school I hid the cat inside my desk. Of course, the Brother heard the cat and seemed angry that I had done this mischief and so he asked – why? I responded that it was his fault because I needed the cat's help with the rats in the dungeon. Everything had gone wrong that day because when our neighbor had seen me take the cat, my father was called at work. He came to the school and while the Brother was discovering the cat inside my desk, the Head Brother was talking to my father and then we all met in his office. While in that office my father found out that I had gotten into trouble the day before and I had said nothing about it – I was speechless and very scared. Suddenly they pronounced that no further disciplinary action would be taken against me because I had suffered enough already. I did have to apologize to our neighbor and promise I would never do it again.

Remembering this event, just before I closed my eyes in my bed in Totowa, New Jersey, I thought, "this discipline business is not easy – how to be fair?"

During the two weeks I was at the orphanage I had no run-ins with "Sister Lefty." I played basketball, baseball and often spoke with a couple of the other boys. One of them, whose parents had both died, often cried at night, and sometimes during the day he seemed angry. He was one of the boys involved in the fight that first night. I wished I could do something for him. I missed my mom and dad terribly and grew increasingly worried and scared because I had not spoken with dad since we said good-bye at the airport in Newark. I did not know if he was okay. If something happened to him, what would happen to me?

Looking back on it now, I see that as very selfish of me, but that was my thinking. I was growing sadder by the day and wondered how these other boys handled the fact that their parents either did not want them or they had no parents. The sisters who ran the orphanage were nice, even "Lefty" when you got on her good side, but I was getting more and more down in my spirits – once again I felt isolated and powerless.

Suddenly one sunny, beautiful day towards the end of June 1962, I was called to the office. It seemed to me that more often than not a call to the office meant bad news instead of good news, so I worried as I headed to the office; I was not sure of anything anymore. Would my dad be there to visit me? Or was this a summons to tell me something had happened to him? Maybe I had done something wrong and would experience firsthand the swift justice of Sister Lefty.

When I stepped inside Mother Superior's office there were two tall people there who I had never seen before. They were introduced to me as Mr. and Mrs. Mulvihill, and I was told that they wanted me to go to their home – if I wanted to. I was ready to break out of the orphanage, as long as my father would know where to find me. Also, I saw something very warm about Mr. and Mrs. Mulvihill. They looked into my eyes with slight but unforced smiles, and Mrs. Mulvihill asked me to come with them. They had children of their own, she told me, and I would be able to play with them. They said that my dad could visit and that I could be with them until my dad was ready to take me to our new home with him. I had met a lot of new people in the past few months, and I was developing a feeling or instinct about people and whether they appeared to be sincere or not. I liked what I saw, and I was sold! I insisted to Mother Superior that my father be informed where I was going; she smiled back and agreed. I have never, ever regretted going with the Mulvihills. I learned so much from them in such a brief period of time that I was in their home from June to August 1962, just before school started.

We left the orphanage that morning. The drive to their home was short, and I looked out the window and saw a very nice area; beautiful landscaped homes, trees, green vegetation. I felt very comfortable and wanted to meet their children. I wondered why the Mulvihills chose me, and I felt lucky for the first time in quite a while.

When I arrived at their home that day I did not speak any English. "Hi, my name is Aldo" was it for me. I did not know how to ask where was the bathroom, and I needed it! I finally made my request understood. It was soon after I had used the bathroom I realized that while the Mulvihills had mentioned that they had children, they hadn't told me how many. The household included eight children ranging in age from 12 years old to six months! Were they crazy? Weren't eight enough? How could they justify me, another one, and number 9?

The 12-year-old was Joe, the 6-month-old was Steve, and in between were five girls, one other boy and me. I had been a single child for 11-plus years, and now as I turned 12 I was in the midst of eight other children – another adventure in my year of adventures! In three years, since January 1959, from the time I was nine until the time I was 12 years old, I had lived a lifetime of adventures complete with terrifying thoughts of loneliness, failure, death, the end of friendships and uncertain unimaginable outcomes of futures yet to come.

Now, even though my future with my parents remained uncertain, I was being given the gift of a summer as a regular child – for a change! I regret not ever telling Mrs. Mulvihill exactly what that summer truly meant to me; very possibly my salvation because, even as young as I was, I did not know how much more

I could take.

My summer of '62 was just what I needed. Earlier I felt as if I had been blindfolded and was being just led around by others. Now I experienced a carefree summer in Wayne, New Jersey, in a lovely neighborhood with an above-ground pool, which we all greatly enjoyed. My dad did get in touch with us, and he and his friends, including my uncle, came to see me a few times. That was the only thing I missed – being with my dad and my mom. But since my dad was here and he was working hard, I remained focused on starting school in Union City where he lived – even though neither he nor the Mulvihills knew this yet.

We had many great times that summer. One weekend we all piled into the Mulvihills' Volkswagen mini-wagon, and they took us to a lake. We spent a great day swimming and playing. Joe played Little League baseball, and the whole family went to watch the games. I wanted to play but it was too late to join, but we played baseball and basketball in the neighborhood. When my birthday came, July 11, my dad arrived to celebrate it. What a wonderful birthday it was for me that summer day. I now knew my dad could find me and yes, he explained he had a job and an apartment and he was saving to bring me to live with him before the start of school in September. This was by far my best birthday and birthday present in a long time!

My dad was driven to the Mulvihills' by my Aunt Felicia and my Uncle Higinio Paz. Higinio was my mom's brother. He was the uncle I mentioned lived in New Jersey – in North Bergen at that time. Higinio would later become very influential in my life, and I would learn a great deal about my family from him. He died in on July 23, 2011, at the age of 97. When he was 95, my son, Aldo, Jr., and I took him to Cuba for the first time in decades and for the last time, to say his good-byes to the rest of the family there.

On the home front life was very interesting with the Mulvihills. I will never forget Mrs. Mulvihill's battles with me over my craving for sugar – yes, I was out of control; I used to put sugar on Frosted Flakes! What was worse is that some of the other children started to imitate me and that drove Mrs. Mulvihill semi-insane. I was introduced to pizza, and I loved it. Hot dogs, hamburgers! What amazed me was how both parents handled all nine of us every day. It made me realize anything was possible!

It is important for me to repeat that the one thing I regret not telling Mrs. Mulvihill before she passed on was how influential she and her husband were on my future life. Not just for having given me the summer I needed, but as a child in their family I realized that that was the way I wanted to someday have my children feel, as a family unit loved and cared for, where the parents' behavior would set an example for them as to how to lead their life.

Of course, I later also realized that even if one chooses not to marry, as long as one helps and brings comfort to others, one feels so fulfilled and at peace – one experiences a state of true happiness that way. It was while I stayed with the Mulvihills that I first experienced the American dream, and I realized that it was hard work to make it happen but I wanted it – this was the type of life my parents had sacrificed for, why they sent me out of Cuba, so that I could have the opportunity to become what I wanted to be. At age 12, having been blindly led through this adventure, I now had an idea of what I wanted to work for. This wonderful family provided me with a slight vision, which I would later bring into focus. How was this possible? Had my terrible experiences actually benefitted me so I could realize this? The Mulvihills taught me by example to give of oneself for others, to not be afraid to do what one thinks is the right thing to do and commit one's entire being to that endeavor. These few months were an illustration of how good things can come out of bad. One of those good things was the new confidence that I was learning to have in myself and my judgments.

After I went to live with my dad in Union City at the end of the summer of 1962, I visited the Mulvihills, at first regularly, then less frequently, but we kept in touch at least by Christmas card every year. In 2010, Mrs. Lee Mulvihill passed away – the passing of a marvelous and very human, human being. She impacted everyone who knew her in a very permanent way, and in the less than three months I was in her home, she and her husband made a lifelong impression on me, merely by the example that they lived every day.

After Mrs. Mulvihill passed away her husband, Bob, shared with me not just how, but why, they took me in that summer. Bob and Lee were attending their usual Mass one Sunday in early 1962, when the priest announced about the Pedro Pan flights. He said there was a need for Cuban children to be taken in by anyone who could do so. On the way home, Lee told Bob that they must do their part and take a Cuban child in. Bob responded, "Yes dear, we only have eight," and sometime later I was the lucky child to be taken in by them.

Chapter 5: Higinio

Who and what is a leader? Are there different types of leaders? What makes a person a good and effective leader? Can a leader be effective but still not be a good leader for me? Do we need role models? What should we expect from our leaders and role models?

When I was 12 years old I did not ask these specific questions, but given the thoughts and questions that I had, I could have been asking them. In time, the answers became much easier when it sank into me that none of us is perfect; that we all have strengths and weaknesses. We can better our lives or make them worse depending on how we react to what happens to us in our lives. We need to understand that life is beautiful, but it can be trying at times. Until we can understand and accept these conditions, we do not possess the capabilities to live a fulfilling life. We cannot bring a smile to another person's face until we begin to care and think about others, and we are just not capable of doing that until we have accepted ourselves, our life condition, and learn what we can and cannot change and how to adapt to those things that we cannot change. We cannot accept ourselves until we have an outlook that welcomes life and its gifts and trials as opportunities that drive us and strengthen us and give us a vision of our tomorrows.

I have always needed role models. I learn by observing others – what they do correctly and what they do wrong. I have come to understand that my future is best served by learning from the people in my life what I should do and not do; and yes, I have also learned the hard way by trial and error. I am an extrovert, and listening is not a trait that comes naturally to an extrovert. My children, both when they were younger and as adults, would tell me "you're not listening to me." I have learned from them and from many others that the hardest thing I must do is to listen. To me, a role model is a leader, a person who cares about others and offers a vision for himself or herself and others; a person who feels comfortable with himself or herself about who he or she is. To me, those role models are people who have suffered from what life brings to them and cares for others. I admire their skills and the style with which they have confronted those challenges while still managing to retain a positive outlook on life.

***

Most families have a matriarch or a patriarch who is not only an authority figure but is also often asked for advice. It is not unusual for these individuals (on their own or when prodded by others) to step into family squabbles and mediate matters. Such status is generally attained either because the person has a controlling personality or because the person is a natural leader and the role is thrust upon this person by other family members. As any other leader, such individuals can either bring benefits to others or be a destructive force.

I was blessed in being part of two families – my mom's and my dad's, where I saw two such leaders. Interestingly, neither one liked the other. My grandmother, Manuela or Nenena, was the matriarch of my dad's family, while my mom's brother, Higinio, was the patriarch of her side of the family. Abuela was a very strong-willed woman. She and my grandfather had two children: my dad and my Aunt Silvia, who now lives in Spain with her husband and all but one of her children. After my parents divorced Abuela took care of me since my dad had custody of me. She loved me very much and understood and respected my parents' wishes that I leave Cuba. However, because she never showed any respect for my mother and not only played a role in my parents' divorce, but later tried to pull me away from my mother, I eventually grew to believe she just wanted to control her family and have them all behave exactly as she wanted. And I was not going to have that.

In contrast to Abuela, there was Higinio Paz, the patriarch of my mother's family. Born on January 11, 1914, in Cardenas, Matanzas, Cuba, he moved to New Jersey in 1957. He was the second oldest of nine brothers and sisters – one died as an infant. They were born into extreme poverty. Higinio never went past the sixth grade in school because at age 10 he started to help support that growing family.

At the age of 17, Higinio became extremely upset at his father when he learned that his mother was pregnant with her ninth child. After all, Higinio had been working for six years to help support his parents and six brothers and sisters. But when he learned that his parents were considering aborting that child, Higinio and his father had a huge fight. He even promised to cut off his father's "pinga" if he were to make another baby. But he also promised to be responsible for and care for this new child if his mother did not abort it. Higinio promised to care for this child into adulthood, or if the child turned out to be a girl, he would not marry until the child married. That child was my mother, and I was 13 years old when I learned of the role my uncle played in my existence. Higinio did not marry until after my mom married my dad, and while he officially never had a son or daughter, he was a father and grandfather to all of his many nieces and nephews. Father's Day was always his day also.

While in Cuba, moving from job to job, finding work

My uncle, Higinio Paz, shown on the left as a young man in Cuba. Many decades later, at age 95, he returned to Cuba. Not only did he still have the same suit, he could still wear it!

for his brothers and taking care of his sisters, Higinio became the person everyone went to for advice and to solve their problems. I think just as a break from all his family in Cuba, Higinio became very involved in civic and political matters, finding solutions for friends and strangers just as he did for his family. Higinio resolved all his family's problems, from clashes with the law when his brothers were caught cheating with married women, to finding jobs for them and eventually purchasing a house for his mom and dad to live in by themselves and away from their adult children. Higinio was not a saint, and he did have a mean streak, particularly when someone he helped failed to understand the lesson and that person would not in turn, help others or when he was disappointed by those he helped in the way they conducted themselves.

Higinio was the uncle who lived in New Jersey, and while at the time I did not know all this about him, he was the family member I wanted to be near when I fought not to be sent to New Mexico from Florida. After I moved to New Jersey I learned that Higinio had left Cuba for political reasons, running to save his life. During the Fulgencio Batista government he had been declared persona non grata. And while you might think that would have made him popular with the next regime, he was also not welcomed by the insurgents headed by Fidel Castro.

Higinio was a union activist who stood up to the Batista dictatorship and fought for justice and benefits and rights for the abused, hardworking and underpaid Cuban man and woman. However, when the Communists wanted to infiltrate the workers' unions to overthrow the government, he strongly opposed them because he felt that Communism was not the answer to the problems of the Cuban working force. During World War II he served at the United States Naval base in Guantanamo, Cuba, and loaded merchant ships carrying war supplies to our allies across the Atlantic Ocean. After World War II there was increased violence in which he was directly involved, and after seeing several of his close associates assassinated and learning that he was next, he and his wife left Cuba and moved to New York/New Jersey. He worked every menial job possible, from dishwasher to laundry worker to clothing pressman. Eventually he opened a business in Union City on 35th street right off the main avenue, Bergenline Avenue, under the name "The 512" – the number of the building. My aunt, his wife, suffered from diabetes during a time when nothing much could be done, and after she had several amputations, he sold the business, retired and took care of his wife until she died in Florida. He then returned to New Jersey and lived his days close to us. He died on July 23, 2011, at the age of 97.

Family chemistry at times can be a volatile, flammable and irreversible condition. In my case, two families, each with strong family leaders – Manuela, my Abuela, and Higinio – provided me with some of the most depressing and desperate moments in my life. Somehow without too much thought and out of sheer desperation, I became determined not to allow either of them to control me. I knew this wouldn't be easy – Abuela took care of me and did it well, and Higinio was responsible for my mother having survived into infancy and for her support and care until she married my dad. Neither Abuela nor Higinio liked each other. Abuela thought my mom did not fit the mold of a traditional wife because she was a beautician and businesswoman; she did not seem to understand that my mom, like her brothers and sisters, had learned from Higinio that it was honorable to work and do the best you could do and therefore she would not give up her work as a beautician and artist.

Higinio, on the other hand, did not like my grandmother because he considered her meddlesome and strong-willed. Neither Abuela nor Higinio realized how much alike they were. Higinio also did not like my dad very much because he considered him too weak to stand up to his mother. Interestingly, although my mom and dad were strong enough to get married despite controversy and disapproval, eventually they proved not to be strong enough to stand up to Abuela. Their marriage lasted only eight years, from 1949 to 1957.

So, how did I, the child of two people who were not particularly strong and who were unwilling to shield me from the conflicting influences of two tough and controlling people, Abuela and Uncle Higinio, survive to establish respectful relationships with both of them? The answer to this question has occupied considerable interest on my part; and although my answer has changed from time to time, I realize that I learned at an early age that standing up to them was less stressful and more productive for me than trying to satisfy their competing and opposite interests.

From the time when my grandmother moved to the United States until her death in the early 1980s, I always worked to have close relationships with both of these influential relations. As a teenager, the first step I took was to make it known to each that I was not going to accept criticism about my parents. I needed to make sure that I was not going to be pulled apart by the two sides of my family, as I had been as a child in Cuba after their divorce. I decided that I would wait until the occasion rose, and in the meantime, I would not force the issue. I was right – although Higinio was more subtle, his first attempt was to exclude my dad when he invited me to visit him and my aunt. After the third time it happened, just prior to Christmas 1962, I firmly told him that if my dad was not invited I would not come. At 12 years old I had started to learn that I was in more control of outcomes if I could anticipate how people might react. Just the fact that I was able to control the outcome of events and the behavior of others made me feel grown up. Learning to think about possibilities and alternatives was not easy, but gaining the desired outcomes made it worthwhile and gave me confidence and strength. I was ready to confront Abuela when she arrived with my grandfather in Union City several years later.

Today I firmly believe three things: One – nothing happens to us for which we are not prepared to endure. Two – when facing what seems an overwhelming situation we have two alternatives – give up or overcome. Three – although it appears that giving up is the easiest way out, it is not! There is so much more at stake. Meeting a challenge head-on and overcoming the adversity is so invigorating and rejuvenating that the effects are empowering life altering moments.

By mid- to late August 1962, seven months after I left my native country, I had endured fear for myself and my mom and dad, illness, loneliness, desperation and an attempt to be sent to a place I did not want to go. Now I was again ready to put all my strength on the line and to be uncompromising. Mr. and Mrs. Mulvihill wanted me to stay with them during the 1962-63 school year; the priest in charge of my case, as well as the Mulvihills, wanted to give my dad a year to get on his feet financially and believed I would be better immersed in the American way of life by my staying with the Mulvihills. My uncle and my mom also wanted me to stay. I did not.

I had planned that by the end of the summer I would be united with my dad. However, unlike in Florida when I took a tantrum, now I asked questions – my dad had a job and an apartment, why was that not enough? Why would I not do just as well in a school in Union City as in Wayne? My dad's apartment was a small studio room, why would I not be able to share it? Why would I not have the support of caring individuals since Higinio would be closer and the Mulvihills would also be available? To the priest I asked, why would the church of

St. Michael's in Union City not be good enough for me to attend? Well, in one week I was registered at St. Michael's school in the sixth grade, moved in with my dad and was feeling extremely empowered to have thought through the details the adults would be worried about and to have addressed them as logically as I could. I persevered and did not compromise on what I ultimately wanted. I have never regretted that move.

Higinio became incredibly helpful and influential in our lives. I came to trust him greatly. He found my dad a part-time job when he needed it at one point when my dad had lost his job. My dad and I spent most Sundays with Higinio and my aunt; we had lunch there, we talked, we met their friends and I played with their friends' children. Sundays became a day I looked forward to. In talking with my aunt I learned much about her and Higinio's experiences and sacrifices when they first came to the United States in 1957.

Higinio was not much of a talker. He was a businessman, and when he spoke with me it was about the work ethic, what it meant to be a man and what he was working at – first pressing clothes and then working on consignment, selling women's clothes. When I asked him why not men's clothes, and he would say "clothes look better on a woman," and wink an eye at me. My mother had warned me about Higinio's liberties with the opposite sex, and frankly I was quite interested in listening to those stories. As I got older we talked about women and life. However, one thing he would always repeat, "It is not the pants that make a man, it is the way he behaves." He used to remind me that although no one is perfect, I should do all I could to never hurt anyone, especially my family. Our strength was in our family, he would remind me. At times, I didn't know exactly what role Higinio was playing in my life; he acted and spoke like my grandfather, my dad and even my mother. One thing he confided in me when I turned 13: how impressed he was when I changed everyone's mind a year earlier when I came to live with my dad. He added that I should never forget what worked in getting my way in life. Was this the same man my mom had warned me about?

I saw Higinio and my aunt endure tremendous suffering when my aunt battled diabetes and she did not take sufficient care of her condition. My aunt never trusted Higinio with the other ladies, and she suffered when first some of her toes and then her legs had to be amputated after complications. Higinio eventually sold the business he had worked so hard to establish and moved with my aunt to Florida where she wanted to spend her remaining days close to her family. After much suffering she passed away. Higinio was in his late 60s and moved back to New Jersey, living in different places before moving to North Bergen.

Higinio also endured the death of all his brothers and sisters, including my mom, and close to the end of his own life he experienced a very difficult situation with a very close family member who never again spoke to him. Although Higinio later experienced loneliness, he always had a positive outlook on life, joked and laughed, made others laugh and just loved life. He was 84 years old when one day he angrily called me to complain that he had just caught his girlfriend cheating on him. His girlfriend was aged 43 at the time, and married. He had hidden a tape recorder by his phone and had recorded her calling another man to arrange a date with him. The words just rolled out of my mouth. "She is cheating on her husband with you and you are worried she is cheating on you with someone else? And how old did you say she was?"

Still, I respected Higinio's wisdom and made sure that as my son grew up he had the same opportunity that I had had, several decades earlier, to have many conversations with his great-uncle and learn from his wisdom. When Higinio was 95, my son and one of my daughters suggested that we take Higinio back to Cuba

The family home, 40 years later. I was sad to see how rundown it appeared, but I did find a neighbor who remembered my family.

to celebrate his 95th birthday and see the family for the last time. My son, Higinio and I spent two weeks together in Cuba traveling to La Habana and to Cardenas, where he was born and grew up, as well as to Varadero Beach.

While in La Habana, we also visited the neighborhood I grew up in and from where I left Cuba in 1962, 47 years earlier. In September 2009, sitting next to Higinio, as the plane flew over the green covered island of Cuba, I remembered my thoughts when I left it as a child, "will I ever see Cuba again?" I don't remember breathing and thought "I am back, what will I find when we land?" I took it all in. That feeling was matched only when seeing the neighborhood I grew up in – walking on the street I used to race on my bike; standing in front of what it used to be my home, looking at the other houses and streets badly maintained. In silence, my eyes swelled up. Days later in Cardenas where we were staying with relatives, when speaking with my son about why I did not visit the tomb of my other grandmother, it hit me. I could no longer hold it back any more and I cried. Seeing my family and Cuba in these conditions was too much for me, I thought.

This trip energized Higinio like nothing else could have, and he even spoke about returning for his 100th birthday. To me, it once again reinforced my parents' sacrifice, and it gave me closure. Everything comes to us in life sooner or later, and there is nothing like being aware of it when it happens.

Chapter 6:
New Experiences

Talk about being stuck in a time warp. It was 1962, and I was a 13-year-old immigrant Cuban boy in New Jersey. But even as I experienced culture shock, I also learned I was not the only one. In 1962, Union City, New Jersey, was a predominantly Italian town, and residents started to look at a new type of immigrant, Hispanics, mostly Cubans, and were curious about those of us who were moving into Union City. But in September 1962, I went back to school full-time for the first time in almost a year, since my parents had taken me out of school in Cuba in late 1961. When in school, it is every child's dream to not go, but once it was taken away from me, in a strange way, I missed it. I had always enjoyed learning, and I enjoyed making new friends and playing with other children my age. School offered me all those possibilities.

The classes at St. Michael's School in Union City, were, of course, held in English. I was nervous about this, but amazingly, I soon realized that thanks to spending the summer with the Mulvihill family, I now spoke English quite well. I also found that although the nuns who taught us were firm and strong disciplinarians, the class atmosphere was not as charged as it had been in Cuba where I had felt compelled to borrow a cat to defend myself against the unknown. Nor did I feel as pressured to perform in the kind of weekly tests and rankings that had been a hallmark of the school in Cuba. All of these differences meant I felt quite comfortable in this new classroom environment.

I was not the only Spanish speaking student. I soon met two other students, and I noted that they did not speak English as well as I did. Jose Rodriguez and Gonzalo Alonso had both arrived in the United States from Cuba with their parents. Jose and his father had somehow been able to come to the States via another country. I don't remember Gonzalo's story, but they both had experienced hardship and confusion in leaving Cuba that was made worse by their families' uncertainty as to how they would actually make it to the United States. After getting to know them and learning about their different experiences in leaving Cuba, I felt quite lucky. My parents had prepared me as well as they could for the uncertainties of what would happen to me while traveling alone, and everything I had experienced in the United States since arriving several months before had also prepared me well for my role as a student in a new school with a new language and new culture.

At times the nuns embarrassed me, particularly when they used me as a model with other students who failed to perform up to their standards. The nuns would point to me and tell everyone how well I was performing even though I had never attended school in the United States, and mention that just a few months before I hadn't even been able to speak the language.

When a student failed to live up to their expectations, the nuns would look at the student and the rest of the class and say, "Aldo has not been in this country one year yet and see the grade he got and he just learned to speak our language...you should do better."

This happened several times and usually when I least expected it. I was very upset at the nuns; I wanted to make friends and blend in as just another student. The nuns had no idea of how school in Cuba had prepared me; nor did they understand my need to make friends and just be like any other student. Besides, I never considered that my experiences made me better than anyone else. We were different, but we were all in the same boat.

My first winter in Union City was filled with new experiences for me. My dad and I had a small one-room apartment in a two-family house on West Avenue between 25th and 26th Streets. My school was twelve blocks away, and as I have told my children, in cold or hot weather, in rain or snow, I always walked to and from school – uphill both ways. My days were simple: I got up early in the morning, walked to school, then returned home to our apartment. A few hours later, about the time I finished my homework, my dad would come home from work. We made arrangements to have a restaurant send us the dinner meal under a program called "cantina." Each week we would decide what we wanted to eat, and they would deliver the items in metal containers, called "cantinas." We would eat dinner in our apartment, wash these containers and return them the next day when the restaurant delivered our next meal.

After dinner, if I had completed my homework, I was allowed to play with my friends for an hour or two. One day in late October, as I walked to school, something began to fall from the sky. For the first time in my life I saw snow! The light flurries and the few flakes that began to cover the sidewalks made walking slippery and strange to me, but I just loved seeing it, touching it and walking on it. I smiled and hoped for more – a lot more snow. Of course, I was also learning about fall weather, and I did not enjoy the cold or wearing coats everywhere. In Cuba the coldest it ever got was in February, when occasionally one needed a light sweater.

But there was even more to learn about American culture. At the end of October, I enjoyed my first Halloween, which had not been celebrated in Cuba. At first, I could not understand why my friends were so excited about dressing up in costumes, going door to door saying "trick or treat."

"What does trick or treat mean?" I asked.

It means "give me a treat or I will give you a trick."

How could we do this without getting into trouble? I wondered. So I innocently asked, "Ok, if someone doesn't give us something, what will we do to them?"

My friends could not agree. "Well how about throwing eggs at their door or scaring them the next time they open their door" was one suggestion. Another friend even proposed painting their front doors. But of course, on Halloween night I found that asking and getting candy was fun, and since we were never refused, there was no need to think up tricks.

As soon as Halloween was over November arrived, bringing talk of a new holiday, Thanksgiving, and all of my new friends were looking forward to it. This was another holiday not celebrated in Cuba. Winter was on its way, school had been in session for just two months and already I had experienced two new holidays. I was really enjoying my newfound culture! When I realized that Thanksgiving Day stemmed from the first pilgrims to this country thanking God and our Native Americans for surviving their first winter in the New World, I felt a unique connection to this day. I have come to think of

Thanksgiving as a holiday of particular interest to new immigrants, and for all of us it is a day to give thanks for family and friends, for having shared life with those who are no longer with us and thanks for all the challenges and opportunities that life brings us all.

But on this first Thanksgiving in the United States, my dad was not too excited. He had just agreed to take on a huge and challenging responsibility, both financial and in other ways: me. While I was asking questions about my new culture and events that had so far been pleasant, he saw one more thing he needed to spend money on. His answer to my questions was usually, "We cannot afford that."

Right after Thanksgiving, Christmas started to come alive – what a great time of the year! I was mixed up and guilty about how I felt. I missed my mom a lot, but for the first time in a couple of years I also felt the joy of Christmas. What joy I felt! I wrote my mom in Cuba of all that was taking place, how I felt, and that I was sorry that even though she was not with me, I was happy. I confessed to her that I felt guilty about my happiness, that I was so excited even though she was not there to experience it all with me. I told her how much I worried that I was losing my love for her and that I missed her very much and missed the opportunity to share all this with her. Weeks later, after Christmas, a letter arrived reassuring me that she and my dad had sent me out of Cuba so that I could feel happy and excited, so that I didn't have to live in fear, and that as long as I was happy, she was happy, because I was letting her know that her sacrifice as a mother had been successful. She told me not to feel guilty about being happy and asked me to continue to share my feelings with her. That would be how I showed her that I love her, the rope that would keep us connected. Her letter made me feel so good. My mom always made me feel important and always trusted and reminded me that I had already grown and experienced so much. By trusting in my love for her she gave me the confidence to trust in myself, and since I had already shown myself that I could control quite a lot of my environment, I grew more secure and confident.

My mom appeared to be so secure about herself, but I did not know then just how much she was suffering in not being able to be near me. Although I was never much of a writer, my mom had just given me the reason to write to her – to talk about my feelings. That was so much help to me, even though letters to Cuba took about two or three weeks to get there and another two or three weeks from Cuba to the United States.

I enjoyed that first winter so very much. From Monday through Friday was the routine of school, home, homework, playing with friends, speaking with my dad about our future and letters to and from my mom. Both my mom and dad were doing everything possible to make my life what a child's life should be. Actually, I was starting to realize that my mom and dad appeared to get along better now and would actually write to each other. I read those letters when my dad was not home. They talked about focusing on me to make sure that I would be able to function well. As it turned out, the feelings I told my mom, she somehow nicely conveyed to my dad, so he knew what to do for me. I was so surprised because during and after the divorce in Cuba, I was the furthest from their minds when it came to how their behavior was affecting me. Now, I wondered, "Have I actually benefitted from Castro coming to power?"

Later in life and shortly after Christine, my oldest child, was born, my mom, dad and I sat together, alone, and I shared how much more responsibility I felt now that I had Christine. All I wanted to do was to keep a smile on that child's face. My dad looked at me and said, "I am so sorry." My mom looked at him and then at me and added, "Your dad and I are sorry for ignoring you because of our differences. It wasn't until we were faced with the possibility of losing you that we really started thinking about you." Even though I already knew this, because they discussed it in their letters, they cried and so did I.

During that winter, I made three good friends in school. They all lived close by. One was Irish, the other Italian and the third Cuban. Steve McMahon, William (Bill) Madsen and Gonzalo Alonso – I now had American friends, and even though we all eventually attended different high schools, I stayed good friends with two of them for some years before we went our separate ways. That winter, we mostly played indoors due to the weather, but after each snowfall we spent several hours snowball fighting and playing out in the snow.

I was doing very well in school in math, science, geography, religion and history; in fact I was excelling in almost all my subjects. I had had similar courses in Cuba, but there we had also had a course on Civility, or how we should behave in public and act towards our neighbors. For example, standing up in a bus to give a lady or an elderly person your seat and respect for the elderly for their status in life and for what they had done and still had to offer. There were times when, tired of being used as an example by the nuns, I did not try my best and could have earned better grades, but I wanted to make friends, not enemies with my classmates. I felt terrible for not doing my best, and I was troubled for weeks, so I decided to ask my dad about it. A very short conversation ensued.

"I can't stand it when the nuns use me as an example of how the other students should behave, Dad. I have started to purposely answer questions wrong so I won't get the highest grade. I want to make friends and not be treated differently!" I blurted out one evening at our apartment.

My dad stared at me, and I worried he would get angry at not doing my best. Instead, he fired back: "Tell the nuns to stop it ,and if they don't still do your best."

So I did. He gave me a pass, but expected I would always do my best. I didn't waste time in taking care of the problem as my father suggested. Next day before homeroom, I approached the Sister and respectfully but firmly asked, "Please Sister, I need for you to stop holding me up as an example when others get bad grades. I cannot make friends that way."

I repeated these words to each of the two other nuns who taught us, adding that "I have already not done my best in tests just so I would not be singled out." They wanted to know if anyone had threatened me somehow, and since that had not happened I said no. I told them I just did not feel comfortable with being used as an example. Surprisingly, each one smiled at me and never did it again. This became another instance that illustrated for me the need for communication – we need to be sensitive to how others feel, about how our words and actions can affect others. Most of the time when we hurt others, we do so unknowingly. Appropriate communication often can prevent undesired results.

As the winter left and spring came around the corner, the time I spent outdoors playing with my friends increased, and as is normal, their parents wanted to get to know me, just as my dad wanted to know my friends and about their families. Similarly, my friends told me their parents wanted to know about my parents. Neither my friends nor I gave much thought as to why these questions were being asked; however, in the spring of 1963, my dad and I would personally experience prejudice for the first time. My circle of friends had grown to five, and I was truly enjoying myself. One day we were in front of one of their houses. My friend's mother called the other boys inside for snacks and did not invite me in. My friend looked at her and said, "If Aldo does not go inside, none of us are going inside." I was very hurt that my friend's mother felt that way toward me, but I was so glad to see that my friend stood up for me.

My dad realized how really tight things were in that one-room apartment. I could not invite any of my friends over, but since my dad was very good with our finances he said he could afford a bigger apartment. We started looking in the classified section of the newspaper and lined up several apartments close to the school. On a Saturday morning in May we walked to the first address on our list and knocked on the door. There appeared to be no one home; no one answered the door. We knocked on the door of the second address, and when the owner answered, I introduced ourselves because my dad still did not speak English very well. The landlord told us the apartment had just been rented. We went to the third house and knocked on the door.

"What do you want?" the man who opened the door asked.

"We have come to see the apartment you have for rent," I told him.

The man noticed my dad did not speak much English and asked me, "Where is your mother?"

"In Cuba, sir, and she will be with us soon."

"Well go back to Cuba," he barked, and shut the door on our faces. I felt emptiness in my stomach, which immediately turned to anger, and I pounded on his front door once, but my dad acted as if he expected that behavior and gently pulled me away. Although I knew how racially prejudiced this country was to the "Negro," I innocently never understood why anyone would look at another person differently, and did not realize what Blacks in the United States were enduring. Suddenly, however, I had gotten a taste of it, and I was repulsed by that perception and behavior. This man attacked my soul, and for a moment made me feel inferior and inadequate. I certainly was not, and I could not stand that feeling. That experience made me a stronger, more determined and more knowledgeable individual – I have never forgotten how I felt that day.

We stayed at our one-room apartment for another year. However, I soon realized that I was at the start of a cultural revolution that would be encompassing and overreaching. My generation was in training, and we would learn to speak up. What a great time to have been alive. I felt alive! These were transformational moments for all of us. Even my friend's parents, good Catholic, religious people, realized what they had done and later apologized to me. I was never again denied entrance to that home. About five years later, I happened to pass by the address where my dad and I were locked out, and as I walked by I saw a Cuban family come out at the same time the owner who had slammed the door in our faces was going into his home – we are a country of immigrants, and we should never forget that.

On 21st street in Union City, one block west of the main street that was named Bergenline Avenue, about seven blocks from where I lived, St. Michael's monastery and church offered a huge parking lot and grounds with several baskets for playing basketball and a field to play baseball. In the summertime I lived on those courts and fields. I would get up in the morning, have breakfast and meet my friends at the field. All morning we would play basketball, baseball or just hang out and talk. We would go to one of my friends' homes for lunch or my dad would bring some lunch for us, since in one room we could not entertain anyone but ourselves.

Saturday nights were spent with my dad and his friends playing dominoes. I was not allowed to play; they played for quarters, but I learned by watching, and sometimes was bold enough to criticize some of their moves. I was dying to play, but was never allowed because this was an "adult" game. There was plenty of cigar smoking and good fun, yelling and camaraderie. These guys had a great time kicking back after a week of hard work, and I enjoyed being with them. The topic of Cuba was a staple in these conversations.

"Castro will be gone in a year or two," one would say.

Others would differ and suggest, "Unless someone kills him he will be in charge for decades."

They disliked Democrats, because President Kennedy had abandoned our troops at the Bay of Pigs invasion. All of those there, including my father, would promise, "When I become a citizen I will never to vote for a Democrat for President."

They also talked about their experiences with prejudice at work, and how they were passed over for important jobs. These men who got together every Saturday evening were working as dish washers, loading platform workers, janitors or waiters in the United States, while in Cuba they had been doctors and lawyers, teachers and university professors, business owners or bankers, like my father, who was now employed in a factory manufacturing plastic music records.

They all talked about how they planned to work to return to their professions in the United States, but they also said that they would go back to Cuba if Castro was soon "dethroned." Several of them went back to school and worked to get their doctor's certification or lawyer's degrees because Cuba would not provide their credentials. Two of them became lawyers here at age 40. The waiter eventually purchased a restaurant and became very well known for his Cuban cuisine. But during that summer this was the adult talk I was exposed to, and I enjoyed their bravado, their work ethic, their commitment, and I learned from them about perseverance. I started to realize that although these men had been knocked down, they were planning to get up again, and they retained a positive outlook and their humor – they were optimistic, and I enjoyed being in their presence.

After Mass on most Sundays, we would spend the day at my Uncle Higinio's place. Higinio would take time to ask me what I had done and to give me some "words of wisdom," such as "Don't take any crap from anyone. Speak up always; be respectful about it, but don't accept unfair treatment."

"So what did you do this week?" He would often ask me.

"Was it right? Can you do it better? Why? Why not?"

He tried to make me understand that I should always go over what I did to try to learn if things could be done better. Higinio was still behaving like a parent, and I could only imagine how much pressure he had put on my mother when he was raising her. Unbeknownst to me, I was getting an incredible education. Higinio told me that he hoped I would do something worthwhile with my life to carry the family forward. Later, when we would get home from those visits, I would write my mom and tell her how I spent the week, and I would convey messages to her from Higinio or my aunt.

The summer was hot and humid, but since I was never too comfortable with cold, I enjoyed the great weather, the summer, my friends, my age and the adults and caring family members. Although my dad and I could not afford to take a vacation and we stayed in Union City, this time was invaluable to me; I was forming my beliefs.

As the summer came to an end, I was looking forward to school. Starting seventh grade at St. Michael's School was much different than the year before. I knew everyone in class, and had hung out with just about everyone. For homeroom we had another nun, and our class was on the top floor on the 16th street side of the building. This year I knew about Halloween and Thanksgiving, and all was going well. Sometimes I had some difficulties with my classwork, but this just made me work harder. All was going well, although I missed my mom terribly. I was now an altar boy, and I had to serve Mass during the weekdays as well. I was a quick learner, and we had to serve at different times during the day. One week I had the first Mass of the day – 6:30 am. The duty of the altar boy at this Mass was to fill the wine carafe to be used for the rest of the Masses that day. Curiosity got the best of me, and after wondering what the wine would taste like, I tried it, and I liked it – "Good wine the priests drink," I thought. Little did I know that a few of these cups would lead me to try to ring the bells during Mass at different times – oh just to try something new! However, the priest celebrating the Mass failed to accept my creativity, and when bells sounded at the "Dominus Bobiscum" instead of at the consecration, I was summarily dismissed. My behavior was reported to my father, and I was grounded for what, in my opinion, was a very long time – one week.

About a month after my indiscretion, my childhood would once again be dealt a shock of reality. It was after lunch, about 1:30 pm, on November 22, 1963. I was in class, and as the nun turned on the television in our classroom we heard the news that President John Kennedy had been shot and killed. Our teacher began to cry. I remember my shock at hearing that a President of the United States had been assassinated. It did not seem possible. This was the country to which I had come to find freedom. How could something like this happen?

I completely changed at that moment. I was afraid again, and I did not know why. I felt sad, because although my father's friends criticized him, they all saw him as a great President for the United States. But what changed me was the realization that my image of a wholesome United States had been suddenly shattered – there was the presence of evil here, too.

Chapter 7:
Mom Comes Home

I had just turned 15 when I started St. Michael's High School in Union City, in September 1965. The high school was right across the street from the grammar school. By then my dad and I had moved to an apartment in a tenement building of about 20 or so apartments, at 618 22nd Street. We now had a bedroom, living room, kitchen and bathroom. I slept in the bedroom while my dad slept on a sofa bed in the living room sofa until my grandmother and grandfather joined us from Cuba sometime in 1967. Then I shared the bedroom with them. My mom, because she was a business owner in Habana, endured interminable difficulties and insults in order to get the permission required from the Cuban government so she could leave Cuba. She was still there.

Prior to giving her a departure permit, Cuban government officials had to inspect her business to make sure she was not selling the business assets and therefore not "unjustly" profiting from the closing of the business. They inspected her beauty salon and counted hair dryers, rollers, hairpins, everything. A month later they would come back and recount these materials and of course, due to wear and tear or appliances in repair, the numbers would not match. Consequently, the government would deny the permit. After several years of this agony and despair she managed to get her departure and in 1967 arrived in Union City.

I remember so well the day I learned that mom was finally coming to the United States. I was playing in a basketball game at St. Michael's High School gym. I had played on the freshman team, and now was a member of the Junior Varsity High School squad. I knew my dad was proud of me, even though he never came to a game. He worked two jobs and never had the time, so when I spotted him in the stands one day, just before halftime, I was surprised and worried.

Why was he there? I wondered. Who was sick? It had to be bad news for him to come to the school during the day. He should be working.

I watched him anxiously for several minutes, planning to wait to talk to him until the game was over, as I knew he and my coach would want. Finally, several minutes into the second half, I couldn't stand it anymore. I approached him in the stands, and as I came closer he smiled at me, and I knew immediately what his news had to be. My mom was coming.

What a feeling!

"Aldo, she'll be here in a week," he said as I got near enough to hear him over the noise of the crowd.

I hugged and kissed him, "Tell me again, I want to hear it again!"

"Ok, your mom will travel directly to Newark next week. You want to go meet her?"

I cried, and was surprised to notice that he was crying, too, a little. Even though Christmas had just passed, I was now receiving my real present. My parents loved me greatly, and they both did the best they could. These five years had been a bigger ordeal for them than for me. I returned to the game and played with a smile on my face. We won that game – another best day of my life! "I am so lucky," I thought.

That week was the longest week I had ever experienced; finally the day came and we arrived at the Newark Airport in the early evening. My dad, Higinio and my aunt were there with me. My heart was pounding, and when I knew the plane had landed, it seemed to take years! Then I saw her; she was so beautiful, she looked so driven, walking fast, and my eyes welled with tears, I couldn't see very well and my face was soaked. About 50 feet away we locked eyes, and she was also crying, handkerchief in hand. She was just running now, so I ran to her and five years without hugging or being hugged by mom exploded in a deadlock hug that neither one of us wanted to break. I started to tell her how much I loved her, and she softly uttered, "Shhh, shhh, let me just hold you for a moment."

No more words were spoken, but all the words in our letters were present. I don't know how long that hug lasted, but when I looked around there was not a dry eye around us including my dad, uncle, aunt and perfect strangers. On the way back I felt so fulfilled. I, as her son, had years earlier put in the official claim for her; even though I was not yet a United States citizen, I was able to make the request as an exemption under the Cuban immigration rules. I knew I had accomplished something huge. I also wondered how things were going for all those other children who had left Cuba like me –

I said a silent prayer for them to have strength to enjoy life as best they could until they could be reunited with their families, and I thanked God for what was happening to me. I spent that night with mom at Higinio's house, and the sun came up before we slept – I had waited so long for this moment, and it was every bit what I had anticipated and more.

By the time my mom arrived, my life was quite settled, and I made it known to my dad, Abuela and mom, too, that I would not accept nor respect anything or anyone who would attempt to put a wedge between my relationship with my mom or dad. My dad had proven to me that he trusted me and believed in me, and he made me feel important. My grandfather was very proud that I was standing up to Abuela. I had also made that clear to Higinio. Notwithstanding that announcement, I still struggled with how to be fair to each of them. The most important thing to me was their individual happiness; I did not want to dishonor their sacrifice for me.

That first night with mom I gave her no time to rest, but she was just beaming at finally sitting down with me and talking in real time without time limits.

"I want you to tell me everything. Start anywhere and tell me all that is in your mind – the good, the bad, what worries you, "todo" (or everything in Spanish). I have waited to hear your voice and see your face."

For me, opening up was an understatement; I am not sure if and when I stopped to breathe. I gave mom a recap of the last five years, but we concentrated on some of my recent stories, observations, thoughts and worries. I started talking about school.

"I am not sure that I want to remain at St. Michael's High School. I am thinking of going to a public school, Emerson High School."

"Why? I thought you were happy there and that you are doing very well there?"

"Yes, I am doing very well, but I am tired of the discipline and being treated as a child."

Also, we had just learned that no more boys would be entering St. Michael's; we would represent that last graduating class with boys. The high school was turning into an all girls school. I played basketball and ran track, and I was fairly good at both. I enjoyed competing in both sports, but track was going to be eliminated during my junior year since there would not be any other boys accepted.

Mom knew about the time that the man had shut the door on my dad and me, telling us to go back to Cuba. I mentioned to her that I was worried that the parents of one of the girls I attempted to date would not allow her to date me because I was Hispanic. I knew the girl wanted to go out with me, but she said her parents would not let her date yet. I later saw her dating someone else.

"Maybe she lied to you and just really does not want to date you. Have you spoken to her and asked her to explain?" I never had.

Changing the conversation somewhat, I shot back "When I asked dad to lend me $5 to take her to have pizza he told me that if I wanted to date I would have to find a job to pay for it." Mom had agreed with him. "I got a job," I told her. "I worked over the summer painting the fence around St. Michael's Monastery."

I also mentioned that while I was dating other girls during the summer I had met another girl, Cuban, who I liked very much. She came around the Monastery often, and now I was visiting her, since the Cuban custom or tradition that a boy who wanted to date a girl had to see her at her house. If they went out together a chaperone had to accompany them. "I am so confused with Cuban and American dating customs. American girls can go anywhere, but I need a chaperone! I just want to have a good time!"

Even though I had told mom quite a lot via letters, I had never mentioned this female situation involving Cuban and American traditions. Consequently, I don't think mom was very prepared, or at least her own world was rotating at incredible speed that night. "Hijo (son), it seems like your life has suddenly gotten very interesting – follow your instincts but you are very young to be worrying too much about these things. Enjoy your life, but don't hurt anyone" was her advice.

I had no idea of half of what she was telling me, but I was sure that I had my mom back. Even though I was looking for more advice and clarity from her, I realized that compared to when we were in Cuba, where my parents always told me exactly what to do, in the United States they were more trusting of me and my judgment. For starters, I was already working and going to school, since at the end of my freshman year I had gotten a summer job so that I could have some money for myself. I was budgeting my money to last the entire school year. I had decisions to make about whether I would stay at St. Michael's or move to Emerson in my junior year, and I was dating. Mom and dad were looking for me to make my own decisions.

***

My sophomore year at St. Michael's High School was a year of great successes and decisions, and although it did not seem easy at the time, once I determined what I wanted to do, I felt much better. I was torn for some time over the thought of changing schools. I knew that since no more boys would be attending St. Michael's, the basketball team would eventually be just two classes, ours and the current freshman class. We had some very good players, but I worried there would not be enough to field a team, and basketball was my first love. As a freshman I had run track to stay in shape for basketball, but I found I also enjoyed it, and was good at it. Although I did not have too much speed, I had great endurance. I enjoyed running long distances. Early in my freshman year during the 1965 spring track season, we traveled to a meet involving several schools, one of them Essex Catholic. My usual race was the two-mile run. My coach thought I had potential, and I enjoyed running long distance and the tactics involved in this 10- to 12-minute race. I was surprised to see that there were lots of people at this race – maybe I didn't realize how popular track was, I thought. My coach told me that this day I would be running the one-mile event. I had no idea who my competition would be. I was so happy to be on the team, and to compete that I just smiled. "Sure, I'll do my best," I responded. When the turn came for the mile run, I was ready, warmed up and loose. The crowd seemed to have grown, and it looked as if everyone had come just to see this race. "So is the mile run really this popular"? I thought.

We were running on a quarter mile track, which meant that one mile was four times around the track. Back then, a good time for the mile run was five minutes. There were about 11 or 12 of us lined up, ready for the start, and my mind was blank, just listening for the starter's gun to be fired – the gun was fired and off we went. Right from the start I thought something was wrong. Everyone sprinted off the starting line, all running hard – "this is a much different pace than the two-mile pace – I need to run faster," I thought.

Although I was running nearly as fast as I could, I quickly moved to the back of the pack. "Very fast, very fast pace," I worried, my breathing getting heavier as I tried to move up and run even faster, but there was nothing I could do. I was losing control as I had during my first race – a two-mile run where I had placed third

– I was frustrated and worried that I was letting my team down. One more runner passed me, and realized I was third from the rear. I stopped thinking as the first lap was finished. Thinking was getting me nowhere so I ran harder and aimed to catch one runner at a time. I just looked at the person in front of me and went for him. I passed one, then maybe three others. I pushed and pushed myself one, two, three laps. I overtook maybe two more runners, and no one that I passed caught up to me again. I realized that everyone else who was still in front of me was too fast for me, and I was determined not to let anyone behind me pass me again. I tried to see who was leading the race, but I could no longer see him. I was exhausted and could not focus – was I going to pass out? Where is he, the leader? Suddenly, right as we started the fourth lap, there he was, coming up behind me running right by me! He had lapped me! Thankfully, the race ended. I felt terrible. I didn't know if I was going to throw up or pass out, but I was upset and embarrassed to have let my team down. I came in somewhere in sixth place or so. I went right to my coach and told him that if I was that bad I would quit. My coach smiled and kept smiling – that got me angry. "He's laughing at me," I thought, as I ranted and threatened to quit the team.

"You just got lapped by Marty Liquori, you did very well," he told me.

I knew who Marty Liquori was – there were three American high schoolers who would run the mile under four minutes by the time I graduated high school, and Marty Liquori was one of them. Liquori would be a freshman at Villanova in 1968, and go on to the Olympics. In 1967, he ran the mile in 3:59.8 minutes while at Essex Catholic.

"Why didn't you tell me who I was running up against?" I asked seriously.

"Aldo, you need to trust me. You ran a 5:40 mile,

and you're a freshman in your second race!" my coach responded. "You need to not worry about your competition. Run for your team and yourself; if you knew who you were running against you would have given up before you started and never would have pushed so hard – I wanted to find out what you were made of – so know who you are and don't let yourself down."

I went on to have a great year and won my share of races, but I had also found out a little more about who I was and what I needed to do, and I felt so good when I didn't give up. Every time I came close to giving up, I just persevered and found a "second wind," or something happened that appeared to be luck, like one of my opponents would slow down.

My freshman and sophomore years at St. Michael's High School were so much fun. The friends I made were great, my teammates were fantastic, and I was doing well. In basketball, I started on the freshman team, and as a sophomore I started on Junior Varsity, played point guard and enjoyed running the offense. Although I could have been better, I worked hard to improve and had some very good games – I loved and still love the game of basketball. Unlike track, where you compete by yourself as part of the team, in basketball you have to play as a team with other teammates, all the time and at the same time. Where in track you run, and you beat or are beaten by another runner in your race, in basketball you cannot win the game without the other teammates who share that court with you.

Playing sports is very much like living life – you struggle by yourself and together with others, as in the family and in the workplace, sharing the same goals and often the same objectives, and in neither can the idea of giving up be contemplated. If it is considered, it must be immediately dismissed. In my sophomore year, my performance in school, basketball and track improved significantly. I had stepped out of my safety zone and done well. I was trusted by friends and teammates and even teachers. I continued to gain confidence, and I wanted to try other new things. I asked my dad if could take guitar lessons; I was working and had saved some money so I could afford to pay for them, but I didn't have enough money for a guitar.

"Comprame una guitarra, por favor." ("Please buy me the guitar.")

"No, I will not buy you a guitar; I don't want you to learn to play la guitarra."

"¿Porque no?" (Why not?)

"Because if you play the guitar you'll be smoking marijuana." My father was reflecting a common misconception in the 1960s that anyone who learned to play a guitar would join a rock band and ultimately turn to drugs.

Of course, my dad's reasoning did not make sense to me. What ensued was one of those teenager/parent battles of great magnitude, complete with my walking out several times and "running away" to sleep at my mom's. My dad never gave in, I gave up, and to this day I regret not learning to play the guitar – it could have come in so handy with the opposite sex during the years that followed. Why is it that most of the time the biggest disappointments one has must come from a loved one?

As spring of my sophomore year drew near I knew I had to make a decision about school. I did not want to leave the basketball team without another player; it would be needed, particularly in our senior year since there would be no underclass to recruit from. However, staying would mean I could not run track, and I was in shape to run. One incident in early spring made up my mind, and for right or wrong I decided to leave St. Michael's at the end of my sophomore year and enroll in Emerson High School.

In Religion class I sat in the first row on the window side of the class, and every morning as class started we would first stand and pray out loud whatever prayer Sister Ruth wanted us to pray. This one beautiful morning I longed not to be in school. I was suffering from spring fever and stared outside during prayer; standing I could get a great view out the window. I glanced at the windowsill at the plants that Sister Ruth had watered religiously every week during the school year. This day I noticed something strange – the plants had not grown much, in fact, they had not changed at all since the beginning of the year! I took a couple of steps toward them and touched one of the leaves.

"Holy shit!" I screamed. "They're artificial!"

Sister Ruth immediately stopped the prayers and demanded to know who had said that. I raised my hand, and without asking why I had said it, she sent me to the principal's office.

"Why are you here, Aldo?" the principal asked when I sat in front of her. "I was sent for punishment," I said, without hesitation. I had never been punished in the two years I had been in high school. I always behaved well, or maybe I wasn't caught, but this time it was undeniable: I had said "Holy shit" during prayers!

When I acknowledged what I had done and explained the situation, the principal asked me what I thought my punishment should be.

I took responsibility. "I know I have to be punished. I should not have said "Holy" in front of "shit" during prayers," I answered. "But what are you going to do with Sister Ruth? She has been watering artificial plants since September!"

I was not punished for that incident, and I have nothing but fond memories of all the religious, brothers and sisters who taught me. They helped mold me, discipline me and give me a sense of respect for others as well as a sense of personal accountability. But I was a teenager, perhaps overconfident, and I did not completely realize then that we are all human and therefore imperfect. It is in that imperfection that we show our humanity to each other. I could not, at the time, accept the fact that Sister Ruth would be allowed to continue to teach even though she seemed to be unaware that the plants she was watering were artificial. I still think that allowing her to continue to teach was wrong for the students and for Sister Ruth herself, but in the years since I have learned that we all need to recognize each person's contribution in our lives and take the imperfections as a way of acknowledging the humanity in all of us. Since I also recognized that there was nothing I could do to change either the way I felt, or to have Sister Ruth stop teaching, I decided to do the only thing I could to take control of the situation. My years at St. Michael's High School came to an end, and later I missed my classmates and friends.

That summer of 1967, I continued to work at the Monastery, and with my own money I bought my first car, a 1959 red Rambler, and got insurance. That Rambler went with me everywhere. My relationship with the Cuban girl, Lydia, I had met the summer before, became even stronger. She was going to be a freshman at Emerson also, and I looked forward to being with her during school. Still, this Cuban tradition of seeing her only at her home and not being able to date her unless a chaperone was with us failed to make any sense to me. Honestly, if we wanted to have sex we wouldn't do it on the streets.

Imbecile tradition – a fear of what people would say if they saw us together, alone! Ridiculous! If Cuban adults would have stopped thinking about what others would think of them and focused on what young people needed to learn about themselves to become well adjusted and functioning adults, they would have realized that such customs would not work well in this country. This restrictive behavior was a contributing factor to Lydia and I marrying a few years later, when we were still very young. We became engaged, and we married when she was 18 and I was 21 on my 21st birthday, July 11, 1971.

At Emerson, I joined the basketball team and the track team. I spent most of the basketball season waiting to hear whether I could qualify to play, since I had transferred from St. Michael's where I had also played basketball. The rule, designed to discourage competitive recruiting between schools, was that a student had to wait one year after a transfer before playing in the same varsity sport he had played at the previous school. I didn't have that problem with track because St. Michael's eliminated the track team that year. I would not play basketball again, though, because Emerson started a cross-country team and a winter track team which ran indoors, and in my senior year another friend, a junior, and I were selected as team captains. I now consistently ran the two-mile race and was doing quite well, even with injuries to my left hip from running on the indoor track. The indoor track was so small that in a two-mile run it was easy to become dizzy from constantly running to the left. I rested the hip for a while, and the doctor suggested I start practicing again by running to my right. It worked; however, I may have come back a bit too soon because for the rest of my senior year I had discomfort in my hip, and although I set school records in the two miles and won just about all my races, I didn't feel a hundred percent.

During my senior year at Emerson my grades had slipped. My dad would ask, "Well, what are you going to do after graduation?" I had spoken with my track coach, Don Bozzone, about college and possibly a scholarship. My dad told me he could not afford to pay for college for me; he did not understand the scholarship concept and thought that it was not a very smart idea. I had also told him that I wanted to marry Lydia, and if I went away to college I would not be able to marry for a long time. Neither of my parents liked the idea of my marrying so young, but I was also dealing with another unforeseen complication in my life. My mom got married.

The day she remarried I did something that I still regret, and I particularly regret that I never told her I was sorry: I did not attend her wedding. Not being there for her hurt her a lot, and I did not realize it. My dad did not like the fact that she was remarrying, and out of respect for him I did not go to my mom's wedding – I didn't think it through very well.

In my senior year my brother was born, in May of 1969. I was 18, and my younger brother was an infant. I was no longer an only child, and I loved it. He was fantastic, cute and on the chubby side. If I had not run track I, too, would have been a very well rounded ball because mom fed both of her sons very well. Today, my much younger brother, Carlos Miguel Fermin, "Migue," is a doctor, and I am very proud of his accomplishments. He is married to Toni Ann, his partner and best friend and the person I credit with giving him the kind of love most of us need to enable us to make a difference. When Migue was born my mom asked me, "What is a good name for him?" I suggested Miguel, and she wanted Carlos. She gave him Miguel as his middle name, so I always called him by the name I wanted. As a baby he looked strong – "as strong as St. Michael," I thought, and I called him by that name.

At the time, all of these things combined to make my senior year quite difficult. I had very little support from dad about going to college; I had hurt my mom and was coping with a newborn brother. The Cuban dating tradition was making life with Lydia miserable. Go to college? Go for a scholarship? Find work? Plan to marry? Things continued to get more confusing and escalated in significance. Things kept on happening, and I could just not ignore them. In June 1969, school would end for me unless I decided to go to college. Or, I could look for a job and the freedom a steady paycheck promised. These were my two basic decisions, but I felt so overwhelmed that I just wanted to run away and give it all up and do nothing. Even the one thing I enjoyed, running track, I was doing in pain. My grades had slipped – there was very little discipline at Emerson, and I slacked off. I had just failed Trigonometry. I pretty much kept all this to myself, not sharing even with my mom. It seemed to me that my dad was against anything I wanted; I had already hurt my mom, and she now had my baby brother and a business to worry about. I was not about to add to her burden, I had already done that quite well.

My grandmother would wait until my dad was present and ask me why I wanted to get married. "If you get married, who will take care of your father when I die?" she would ask.

"What?!" my brain cried out. My grandfather, as always, sided with me and would whisper, "Do what you want, you're the only sane one in this family." Then, in mid-May of my senior year, fate stepped in. The high school had a visit from a recruiter from the New York Stock Exchange (NYSE). The lady presented a very enticing picture of employment at the NYSE; it provided good pay and the potential for growth and some very interesting benefits such as health care and paying for part of my college tuition.

Suddenly sitting there in class and listening to her speak about stocks and dividends and working on the trading floor where all of this was going on, everything came into focus. It was just like a fast break on the basketball court: I could see the play develop in front of me! I could do it all, and I could make decent money and more if I proved myself. "I will apply for a job at the NYSE...save for a couple of years to get married...no college, no scholarship."

Within a couple of days I took off from school and went to the NYSE – 11 Wall Street, New York, NY, to apply for a job. It was an entry level position: page or trading floor messenger, carrying messages to and from brokers. There were tests I could take after I had worked there for some months, so that I could advance to other positions, and I planned to take all of those tests as soon as I qualified. For me, everything was riding on being hired by the NYSE. I knew I could take care of everything else. When I went to apply for the job I was given a series of math and English tests, which I thought were very easy. A week later, someone from the NYSE called me to say I was hired. I would start my job June 29, 1969, just days after my graduation from Emerson High School. I had made choices, I had compromised, and perhaps I was choosing alternatives not in my best interest – the decision to get married as soon as possible, to go work rather than to attend college. But I knew I could not afford college, I didn't really understand how to pursue a scholarship and in the end, I did the best I could to take advantage of an opportunity when it became available.

Mom and dad were impressed that I was able to get a job at the New York Stock Exchange, in New York. I was glad they were pleased, and I felt confident about the journey I was about to start. Years later my mom and dad told me that neither one had really understood how I made my decisions or figured out what I wanted. "That's okay, neither did I," I told them. "You guys put me in a plane alone so I could have the opportunity to grow up to be what I wanted to be. You taught me to trust that even though I might not know exactly where I was going, if it was the right thing it would work out."

At that time I still had not understood the real meaning of what they did by letting me come, alone, to the United States. I did not understand their sacrifice; my parents were willing to give me up and chance never to see me or be with me again so I could become whoever I wanted to be. Theirs was the most rare and unspoken gift of unconditional love, which would forever affect not only my life but the lives of those not yet born. Such a rare and unselfish gift can only be accepted by dedicating oneself to honoring that gift as best as one is able to do so.

Chapter 8:
It All Works Out

Getting a job was one of the most liberating moments in my life. Life in the 1960s was, in many respects, so different than today. It seemed that we were asked to grow up faster than in current times; that so much more was asked of us, starting with President Kennedy, who had said, "Ask not what your country can do for you, ask what you can do for your country."

We were the generation born after World War II, the offspring of that generation that had given the highest measure of sacrifice for the continuation of our way of life. We were locked in an ever escalating nuclear Cold War with the Soviet Union and against the spread of Communism. This Cold War, however, did not mean that armed conflicts had been eradicated, and people my age were dying in Vietnam every day in an apparent unsolvable military conflict. I had, by this time, chosen to become a United States citizen. That day in 1968, six years after I had come to this country, I stood inside a packed court room in Newark and swore allegiance to my country, the United States of America. An overwhelming sense of responsibility struck me. This was the country in which my parents had placed their trust and dreams, where they had sent their most prized possession – me.

Becoming a citizen also meant that I accepted the responsibility that I might be drafted into the military. We did not have a choice at that time, as young people do today, with an all-volunteer military. We were 17, 18, 19 years old, and almost all of us had already been touched by the war in Vietnam. We knew people who had been drafted, and we knew people who had died in Viet Nam. A friend of mine, the brother of one of my track teammates, had been blown up by a mine and killed while serving in the military there. The consequences of war are always the same, and they include defeat or triumph and loss of precious lives, destruction of loving relationships and unimaginable terror. These long term consequences continue to be very palpable in today's world, and the current violent conflicts should remind us that war is and must be the last resort for self-preservation. Culturally, we must not romanticize war; we must recognize war as a human failure before we can effectively engage our intellect and strength of character. Maybe once we, as a society, learn to regard war as a leader's personal human failure, we might move our culture to regard a more constructive way of resolving our differences as a key component to great leadership.

In contrast to the reality that we were expected to risk our lives for our country if our number was called in the military draft lottery, it was not completely acceptable for a young man or young woman to leave home and make a life on his or her own before getting married. Such departure was viewed upon as an insult to the parents, a rejection of family values that did not speak well of the young person who was leaving or the parents whose child decided to leave. In addition, if you were Hispanic, there were even greater cultural contradictions. You could not date without a chaperone tagging along. But amazingly, 18-year-olds could drink alcohol in most states. At 18, we were old enough to drink, we could vote and we could die for our country, but could not make a life on our own or be trusted to live away from our parents.

These were a few of the societal norms that started a generation-wide cultural rebellion – a good number of us experimented with drugs; we did not treat sex as a taboo, but rather something that was good, loving and natural. Woodstock, culturally, was our statement, our outcry, our way to emphatically say to our elders that life should not be about war and violence, but rather it should be about love, about caring for each other and about having the personal freedom to pursue our lives. Right or wrong, each one of us became accountable for our own actions and personal behavior.

We fought our parents for the right to leave home and become adults as early as possible. In contrast, it seems as if today, our young men and women have more options available to them. There is often an extended young adulthood where college graduates return home, due to economic or career issues. Culturally, they are not locked into just one choice. It is more acceptable for them to choose what is right for them; whether to stay or leave home, whether to marry or not, whether to have children or not. All are socially acceptable. Will all these choices bring better results for future generations? What will be the societal effects of our young adults taking longer to face certain critical responsibilities and issues? Isn't life an incredibly stimulating journey?

In June 1969, just days before high school graduation, I was a very confident 18-year-old. I had worked during the summers since my freshman year. I owned a car, which I had paid for, and I paid for my car insurance. Psychologically, I had not been sheltered by any of my relatives. I had succeeded academically, in sports, in relationships, both of my parents and a set of grandparents had been able to move to the United States, and no one pressured me to take sides with one or the other on family issues. I had good friends, and I was proud to be making some money. I was the product of a broken home and of divorced parents. I had experienced the pains of failure, disappointment, loneliness, desperation, prejudice and family hurt. The hurt had come before the triumph, which was, in part devastating, and in part sobering and humbling. I had taught myself not to have extreme reactions to either failure or success.

Although I was ambitious and expected a lot of myself, I was also careful to be realistic. I did not bargain or sacrifice the dreams that I was working toward. Instead, I usually adjusted or negotiated the time frames for my goals. For example, I wanted to go to college and continue with my education, but I also understood that neither my parents nor I could afford it, so I decided to get on with my life and committed to get to college when I could. I quickly realized that, when making decisions, if I postponed or procrastinated until another day, that next day would only bring more issues to deal with. I learned that the best way to keep my sanity was to figure out which were the most important issues to me, and meet them head on. Addressing and resolving the things that mattered gave me such a natural high, and filled me with a sense of accomplishment and confidence – and when I became aware of that, I decided to always follow that behavior.

As with most of us, I brought both happiness and sadness to my family. I had asked "will you marry me?"

of Lydia, and she had said yes. Was it that I fell in love at a very early age? Or had the personal, social and cultural mores of those days pushed me toward making the decision to marry? Today, I cannot imagine my life without my daughter, Christine, who was born of that marriage. Even though that marriage ended only six years later, getting married at that time was never a mistake; it was a decision that I made with the best of intentions, and while I was in love.

However, nothing compared to how I felt when I was offered a serious job, a responsibility, by strangers who were willing to pay me, to hire me ahead of others, showing they believed in me and my ability to do a good job. This was liberating because it freed me to put my plans for the future into action – to marry, to have a home of my own and to go to college. I could not contain my excitement about working at the New York Stock Exchange. The job gave me the freedom to sail into unknown and uncharted territories. How incredibly exciting and fulfilling it was! Up to this time, no one had shared with me how they had felt when they were first offered a job, so these feelings were very new. I wondered if it was just me who felt this way. Did others actually not realize when happiness struck them? Even some of my dad's friends didn't seem to understand how I felt.

"I will be working at the New York Stock Exchange full time," I told them as I sat in on a game of dominoes one afternoon when they needed a foursome to complete the teams.

"What are you going to be doing?"

"I'll be a messenger working on the trading floor."

"You are just going to be a messenger. You need an education to go beyond that position" was the dry response.

"I will get there." I tried a track analogy. "It doesn't matter where I start, only where I finish, and I will make a difference someday."

What I kept inside me was that a long time before I had dedicated my life to honoring my mom and dad's sacrifice, their unspoken gift in sending me away from them to the United States. There was no way that I would allow those years when my mom suffered alone and my dad, a professional in Cuba, had to recreate himself and work in a factory manufacturing records, to go without meaning. I believed I could do anything I wanted to do, but even that strongly-held conviction was tempered by the fact that I had already learned that there were constraints to that belief. I really wished to play professional basketball, but I realized that certain physical and talent constraints were too much to overcome to reach this goal.

Realistically, however, doing my best and being driven to improve all the time was not hard for me. I always felt bad when, due to disappointment or just feeling sorry for myself, I let up on my drive and enthusiasm. Course correction at those times often came as a result of becoming angry at myself. A swift kick to my ego usually helped me refocus on what I wanted to accomplish, and made me feel better. If I could benefit others in the process, such as my teammates, I felt even better. Slowly, I had realized that making others feel good about themselves made me feel better – selfish of me, wasn't it? Without realizing it, in high school I had developed the basis for what I believe is necessary for anyone to accomplish their objectives: a realistic understanding that life will not present you with anything you cannot handle.

It was 1969, I was 18 years old and as an American citizen I could vote in elections. This was extremely important to me. I felt such a sense of responsibility. In my native Cuba, for centuries people had fought and died for the right to vote and have a voice in their government, something I could now freely exercise. My country was the most powerful country in the world, engaged in fighting my enemy: Communism. I took American citizenship very seriously, and I still fail to understand when fellow citizens fail to vote – the ignorance and arrogance of it all!

Just like most 18-year-olds, I struggled to make sense of politics, the economy, life and religion. Those were, and still are, the main issues of the day. Later that year, on December 1st, the United States, for the first time in 27 years, held a lottery draft for the military. It was necessary, given our increased presence in Vietnam. My birthday was drawn as the 248th number. The concept was that the government would sequentially draft those born on the dates picked in the order determined by the draft lottery. No one knew how deep into that order the government would need to go to reach their draftee quota. Rumor had it the draft would reach the first 150 birthdays in the first quarter of the year.

As soon as the lottery ended, I looked to join the Army Reserves. Even though I was a staunch anti-Communist, I had friends who were already in Vietnam, and increasingly I believed this was perhaps not the place to make the stand against Communism. At the time, I did not feel that the history of events in Vietnam favored our cause. I wanted to join an Army Reserve unit close to where I lived, Union City. Asking questions, I learned that at Caven Point in Jersey City, there was an engineering unit recruiting, so I applied and was subjected to a test of my engineering capabilities. The sergeant came to me after the test was graded and announced in amazement that he had never seen anyone score so low. He rejected me.

"Maybe you missed an answer on the score sheet and that made all the other ones wrong?" I asked, and quickly learned that you never second guess a sergeant.

He pointed to the front door. I headed for that door, which was maybe 50 feet away, and as I opened it to leave I heard him bark, "Martinez!"

"Now what? Further insults?" I thought as I turned around.

"One of my cooks did not reenlist; you want to go in the kitchen?" I served in the U.S. Army Reserve until 1978, when I was honorably discharged before heading to law school.

Religion was another area where, at 18, I was learning to think for myself. I believed that faith means more than just going to Mass on Sundays and praying the traditional prayer. I believed that Jesus died for something more than that. Jesus, being God, had to have been very human, and to have had a very simple message: we need to work to improve the condition of others. Caring for others is the right thing to do. Love is His message, and that message can be conveyed from the heart without pomp and ceremony. My prayers have always been first and foremost a cry for gratitude, a thank you for what happens to me, for what I perceive to be good or bad, because without both I will not enjoy the balance that maintains my focus on what is important in life – the preservation of human dignity in every way it can be experienced. My prayers include a plea for strength to handle my successes and failures with the perspective that they are teaching moments pointing the way to the next steps I must take to improve others' quality of life, and by doing so enriching my life; to show me the way to fulfill all the best that is in me. Finally, I pray for protection for myself and my family so that they will always have the opportunity to realize happiness in its true form.

My political perspective at that time was driven from my experiences in Communist Cuba, and my vote was to be cast for whoever I thought would confront

Communist expansion. Guided by my basic principles of honoring the dignity of every human being, I have wavered, or in today's language flip-flopped. I have voted for people from both political parties and causes on both sides of the political fence, according to what I believe is the best decision given the circumstances at the time and the future consequences of actions taken in the present. My abuela and my mom taught me this, ironically often while they were screaming at me for something I had done. "What were you thinking was going to happen?" they would shout. On the other hand, it felt good to see they agreed on something.

Economic issues and discussions meant nothing to me in 1969; I was just a high school graduate, but I was determined to change, and thought that working at the NYSE was a good start. June 23, 1969, was my first day of work at the NYSE. What an amazing day. I liked to read biographies and books about history, and I was very familiar with the importance of the New York Stock Exchange in the development of the United States, and I was very much aware of the role that the stock market played in allowing corporations to raise capital for their operations.

Simply put, the NYSE is at the heart of our country's growth, and not only was I now part of the American work force, I was working at the NYSE. I was ready for the challenge, and anxious to take the next steps. During my first week at the NYSE I found that by taking a series of tests, not only my salary would increase but so would my responsibilities. Within the first six months I had taken and passed all the tests. I had moved up from Messenger, started to save for the wedding, joined the Army Reserve and realized that if I went to college, depending on my grades, I could get most of my tuition paid by the NYSE. I was headed in the right direction, and my excitement grew every day. I was also learning how trading took place; learning what a good trade was and how not to effect a bad trade. When other traders appeared to game the system, I wondered if there was any oversight of the trading. I asked my supervisor, "How can they get away with this?" He explained that there were people at the NYSE watching what was going on – that job fascinated me, and I wanted to know what I had to do to get involved. I realized that if not noticed, these practices harmed investors. I checked the Human Resources announcements about open positions and realized that a college degree was needed to work in this area. Another piece of the puzzle fell into place. I was going to go to college.

Before going to college there was a detour. In July 1970, after my birthday, I headed to Fort Jackson, South Carolina, for my Reserve training. My engineering unit was sending me to become a soldier and a cook. I spent five months there, the first two or so involved basic training and the remainder for specialized for advanced training – cook school! I went into basic training weighing 125 pounds and running a 5:25 minute mile with my boots on, and when I graduated from cook school in December, I weighed 145 pounds, and it took me almost 7 minutes to run that same mile!

During basic and advanced training I made some very good friends; one was also in the Reserves and went through cook school together. Another went to advanced infantry training after basic training. His training was shorter than mine and completed two weeks earlier. I knew this because I got word that immediately after his training ended he was activated to Viet Nam and was killed after one week there. He was so much smarter than I. In training, when we served "point" during a mock Viet Nam patrol, it was obvious that he had a sixth sense about being in battle, especially compared to mine. As point, I was supposed to identify the enemy on the field – I saw nothing, and the opposing squad picked us off clean, and I was hit with fire from bee-bee guns a half a dozen times before I hit the ground.

When I heard he had been killed, I realized immediately that if I had been sent to Vietnam, the likelihood was I would not have returned. This was the second time I had lost a friend in Vietnam. I was angry and questioned whether we should be there. What was the purpose of fighting a war if we could not invade the enemy territory, North Vietnam? Why were we fighting a war if we were not fighting to win it? I felt so much empathy and pride for our soldiers there, and I felt that politicians were letting them down, and just as important, too many folks at home in the United States were not recognizing the sacrifice these men and women and their families were making. My gut was not settling well on this war, and by now I trusted my gut. I agonized and struggled to find enough information to vote accurately. In the next election, I voted for Nixon because I thought he would end the war.

Our American Democracy is not something to take lightly. Democracy's strength is found in the citizens' desire to not just take a politician at his or her word – take the message from another Republican, President Reagan, when directing himself towards the Soviet Union – "trust and verify." You can trust a politician if you desire, but the integrity of the process calls for verifying his or her statements. Trying to understand the other side of the issue is always a good start. Democracy, to work at its best, demands advanced objective, and educated citizenship. Of course, it helps greatly to read and understand the Declaration of Independence and the U.S. Constitution. In the late 1960s and early 1970s, there was general upheaval in our country; in many ways the people and our leaders did not appear to be headed in the same direction in race relations, foreign involvement and the Vietnam war, domestic and economic concerns.

There was a battle for the hearts and minds of our country's conscience. What were our values as a society? As some have said, history tends to repeat itself, and to me it seems we are experiencing similar effects today. At the core of the argument this time is the dignity of the human being. There is a need for zealous but respectful debate of the issues, not the humiliation of the debater. That is the key to perfecting our hard-fought democratic form of government.

***

Returning from five months in South Carolina, I had to continue to serve a weekend a month as part of the Reserves enlistment, and had to attend two weeks every summer or spring in active duty, often traveling to a neighboring state. The NYSE not only held the position available to me, but allowed me to take the two-week training without impacting my vacation time. For that I was extremely grateful. However, three things occupied my mind when I returned from my training – continued advancement at the NYSE, my wedding and going to college. There were so many other things that were going on, but focusing on a few significant, achievable goals at one time has always worked best for me. Also, each of these objectives came with accompanying issues. As to college, I had to first pay the tuition, and then be reimbursed depending on the grade I received, but I had to decide when I could afford to start, and where to go since I was going to go at night after work. I would have to do a four-year day program in six years at night. This meant the likelihood that I would remain working on the trading floor for the next six years, since most other positions required a college degree. Discussing this with Lydia, she wondered why I wanted to go to college, but we agreed we could afford both the wedding and college if we married on July 11, 1971, and I applied to start at St. Peter's College in Jersey City in September 1971.

I planned to pay for everything because none of the parents were too much in favor of it – Abuela was wondering who would watch out for my dad once I moved out of the apartment – as if I could possibly do anything about what my dad decided to do. I just wanted to leave that apartment and start my own destiny. On top of all the other concerns, no one seemed to be able to afford the wedding. In the end, her parents picked up the cost of the band; my parents could not afford anything. My prediction was correct; I had been saving to pay for my own wedding. This was also a very interesting conflict of traditions – when dating I needed a chaperone even after Lydia and I became engaged, and this tradition had to be upheld even in a country where that was not the tradition. Even though Cuban tradition called for the parents paying for the wedding of their children, that tradition was swiftly sacrificed – this was nothing more than picking and choosing which traditions are convenient and discarding those which are not.

I had realized very early that I needed to become financially independent if I wanted to do things my way. Lydia and I arranged all of the details, the wedding, the honeymoon, the invitations and the list of invitees. We had no one advising us, so at each step we were inventing the wheel. We agreed on the list of invitees. I wanted my dad to be my best man; he agreed, and we invited the friends he wanted to invite. Lydia and I had some difficulty in determining how our invitation should read. Normally, both parents pick up different expenses and both their names are included. I figured that to be fair, since my dad was not contributing anything, he was not going to be included in the invitation. Neither did my mother's name appear on the invitation. When my father's friends started to receive the invitations and he realized his name was not on it, he exploded. "I will not attend this wedding, and I have told my friends that I have not invited them! Who do her parents think they are to appear on the invitation and I do not? I will not stand for this, and I will not be your best man, Find someone else."

I tried to explain that it was my decision, not Lydia's or her parents', and I had decided, based on what I thought was fair.

His response? "Well I don't want anyone to find out I did not pay for anything."

"It's too late for that now, because that is why your name does not appear on the invitation."

My mom was at my wedding; no one from my father's side attended. A good friend of mine since elementary school, Jose Rodriguez, was my best man.

Chapter 9:
One Step At a Tiime

Until our time on this earth ends, whether we are ready for it or not, the future always arrives. It happens to us as a child, a teenager and as an adult.

Some of the questions that inhabit my head from time to time are: Who am I? What am I doing here? What happens next? What do I do now? Sometimes these questions or their answers are devastating if we fear the present or the future. I believe that often, even if I am not consciously aware of these questions, my brain attempts to address them subconsciously, and sometimes the subconscious approach does a better job than the conscious. Either that or ignorance is bliss. I say this because when I started to work at age 18, I had no idea what I wanted to do with my life. I don't remember ever asking, "Who am I?" I just stepped out and headed in the direction that seemed like the right way to go. Standing still was never an option. I stepped into the future in all of the possible directions that my heart told me my mind could stand.

So two years after my high school graduation I had moved within the NYSE as far as I could go without a college degree, I had satisfied my military responsibility as a United States citizen by signing up in the Army Reserve, I had gotten married and I was headed to college for a six-year journey of night classes. Also, in another 15 months, on October 23, 1972, I would start the most significant journey I would ever undertake. I became the father of Christine, my beautiful little girl, my first of four children. I changed completely the moment Christine was born.

When the future arrives it never is as I envision it. Sometimes better and sometimes worse; the difference is that when we imagine the future we experience it in our minds. When the future arrives, we live it. Enjoying that future in the present is very much a part of that journey. The day Christine was born was a day that Lydia and I had been living, enjoying and anticipating for nine months. However, when I was finally able to hold Christine in my arms and look at her, touching and counting fingers and toes and watching all of her expressions, my focus in living changed completely, turning to Christine – what a responsibility at 22 years old! Nothing I had imagined felt like I felt at that moment. The time had arrived to be responsible for someone who could not take care of herself.

At that time, hospitals did not permit fathers to be present in the labor room or during the birth. I took Lydia to St. Mary's Hospital in Hoboken, New Jersey, on the morning of October 23. I wandered the waiting room, wondering what I should do. "It's going to be a while. Go and do what you normally do and be back in the afternoon," a nurse told me. So I went to work and returned at noon, minutes before Christine was born. When I got to the hospital, I went right to the maternity ward.

"My wife, Lydia Martinez, is in labor here. How is she? Can I see her? What is happening?"

"All is going well, and any moment now your baby will be born," the nurse told me.

I stayed in the waiting room. There were other folks there, but I was alone with my thoughts.

"What if something goes wrong with Lydia or the baby?" I worried silently, not wanting to talk to anyone. It seemed like an eternity, but less than an hour passed before a nurse came to get me, asking...Asking! "Would you like to see your wife and baby now?" Talk about a rhetorical question!

Lydia looked happy and tired. "It's a girl, Christine," she said. We had already decided on a name. They brought Christine into the room, and the nurse asked, "Would you like to hold her?" Why so many obvious questions?! I felt like screaming, "Give her to me!" Finally Christine was placed in my arms; the nurse watched me and smiled – no words were spoken, my eyes immediately became glued on her and tears began to slip out of the inner corners of my eyes. I have become very familiar with those tears; they flowed three more times for my other three children, unshakeable and completely destabilizing joy.

As I held Christine, many things raced across my mind; some silly and some life changing. How could I have gone to work? That was wrong. At that moment I realized that not allowing fathers to be part of the birthing process was wrong. I was determined to never again be kept away from the birth of any of my children. My next thought was an affirmation of the direction I was headed. "I need an education to expand my potential and my career, to do the best I can at work and to be a good father and husband." With Christine in my arms I made a silent and very private promise to give my family the best home and life I could provide, and I rededicated myself to the plans I had made.

Life certainly became a lot more interesting and more defining. Of course, the immediate effect of a new baby is lack of sleep for mom and dad, and worry about the child's feeding and health. Hunger, Pampers, heat or cold aside, there are other things a bit more challenging like colic, colds, fevers, ear aches, sinus congestion and flu, which present more difficult situations. Added to that is what to do for the future needs of the child, like education and safety. But the present has to be lived – the present needs to be enjoyed. I would leave home early in the morning for work at the NYSE, and then four days a week go right from work go to college and return home by 9 or 9:30 p.m. I was motivated, very enthusiastic about what I was doing and where I was headed – not easy on Lydia or me. I stayed away from school during the summer, so from June to August I was home by 5:30 p.m. at the latest, except if coworkers and I on Fridays would stop and have a couple of drinks before going home.

Doing this for six years was hard on all of us, and it took a toll on our marriage. Being young means we do dumb, irresponsible things, without thinking about the outcomes, but given my childhood, I had learned that such behavior was not the exclusivity of young people. We, as adults, are also capable of screwing things up. Lydia and I were young, but we were adults. She stayed at home with Christine for some years, and her mom did very well in babysitting when we needed time alone, but Lydia and I began to move in different directions. We started to argue more about relatively insignificant things, and the fights became more frequent. I was starting to have a lesser say in what we would do. She planned things to do with her mom and often I encouraged it, but it got to a point that whenever I wanted to do something her answer was, "No, my mother has other plans."

Lydia also started to work as a teller in a neighboring bank, and perhaps that is part of the reason why she began to think differently. I was pleased she was working; it brought us another needed income, and I thought she could use the time away from Christine. She had at first questioned my attending college and I didn't make too much of it; heck, I also questioned it. Then, three or four years into our marriage I began thinking about law school, and she was not very happy about it. My mom and my grandfather encouraged me, although my father was silent about it. Strangely enough, years later, after my grandmother passed away, I was reviewing her files and documents and found a letter she wrote to me, which she had never mailed. It said that I was wasting my time going to law school, that I would never be a good lawyer or even become a lawyer and that I should stop pursuing it and stay at home. When I found that letter I was already an attorney and was conducting myself quite well. However, at the time, Lydia was firm in saying, "You don't need to go to law school." I had – and still have not – ever told anyone what to do with their life, and I did not react well to others telling me what to do with my life. I wanted and needed encouragement, and I was getting opposition.

A lot of things came to a boiling point as I graduated college in 1977, determined to go to law school. I needed to concentrate, to study for and pass the entrance examination for law school, and that was not an easy task. I could not take it any longer. Our arguments were too frequent, and I did not like what it was doing to us and to Christine, who was not 5 years old yet. I was afraid of how much uglier our relationship could get. At age 27, after six years of marriage, I had failed big time. I walked out on my marriage. My love for Lydia had vanished. Only then did I understand my parents' divorce, but I could not stand the feeling that I had a big responsibility in the failure of my marriage. I had done the last thing I ever wanted to do to Christine: end the very home I promised myself I would provide for her when I first held her in my arms.

At some time or another we all fail. We fail in life, in our jobs, in our personal behaviors. We tend to feel the lesser for it, and to a great extent we should. However, while we experience those failures we should not let those times be wasted and we should learn some lessons. While we cannot change what has happened to us, we can react to these situations, and armed with our knowledge, experience and desire to become stronger and to do the best we can, grow and do it better. Remembering the suffering my parents caused me after they divorced, I quickly consulted a child psychologist as to what I should do and how I should behave to minimize the hurt this development would cause Christine.

Arriving on time at the doctor's office, we greeted each other, and he asked, "Tell me what the problem is." I explained the situation and said, "I come from a broken home. At the age of seven my parents were divorced. I suffered, and they suffered. I became a pawn for the family, and my parents and their troubles. I felt I was being torn apart. I don't want Christine to feel what I felt, and I am seeking guidance on what to do and what not to do so I can prevent or minimize her suffering from what is to come."

He looked at me intently throughout my explanation and without missing a beat said, "Leave her. Leave your wife and Christine forever. Never ask about them and start your life over again; years from now Christine will forget all about you." I could not believe my ears. I was stunned, couldn't muster a word. Never had I even thought about leaving Christine, abandoning her forever! I thought, "My God, if either of my parents had left me when they divorced my soul would have been taken from me. I would have been devastated."

My response to this doctor was simple. "Our session is over – thank you for your time. It is impossible for me to do what you suggest." I left his office without another word being uttered. There was no way that I would leave Christine. So my solution, given everything I had experienced as a child, was to understand that one of the parents had to take the initiative and responsibility for the sake of the child. "I need to swallow my pride to a great extent in the future with respect to what is yet to come, and always let my love for Christine guide my actions." And swallow my pride I did; however, love does conquer all.

Swallowing my pride was so much easier than I thought it would be. I eventually realized that my course of action did work. Years later, I am convinced that that doctor in his incredibly inept approach did more to help me to convince myself of what I needed to do than anyone could have at the time. I did not challenge Lydia having custody of Christine, but I did see her every other weekend and for two weeks during the summer, and our love, Christine's and mine, flourished over the years.

Eventually, in 1979, after our divorce, I married again. My wife, Susan, and I have now been very happily married for 32 years. Lydia also married Artie, who was a fantastic stepfather to Christine and with whom I got along very well. Lydia had two boys from that marriage, and years later she divorced Artie and married David, with whom she had a very bright and wonderful son. Today Christine has two sisters and a brother from our side and three brothers from her mom's side, totaling four brothers and two sisters. We all are civil to each other. Christine is an attorney, married to a wonderful man, a great son-in-law, and they have two beautiful children, Simon and Samantha. Life is a beautiful but rocky journey. At some point our future always becomes our present, and we have more power to shape it than we think. We just need to come to know what love is and trust in our human capacity to love – the well-being and happiness of my loved ones became my focus and my drive to have confidence in my need to love and be loved.

***

I attended St. Peter's College in Jersey City, New Jersey, the Jesuit college of New Jersey, and in 1977 graduated from the evening division. When I graduated, I was president of what was then known as the Evening Division Student Organization (EDSO). I first met Susan at St. Peter's. She graduated there in 1980, and when I met her she was the Secretary of EDSO. She also worked in New York two blocks from the NYSE. St. Peter's College became very special to me. Studying there facilitated my development and convictions about behavior that became the creed I live by: See God in my fellow human beings, true happiness only comes from benefitting others, and do not be afraid to love – without love there is no life.

When Susan and I were dating, I told her that I was afraid to get married again. I did not know if I was marrying material. After I separated from Lydia I did not place much value on my ability to love. I was hurt, wounded and afraid to take any step that would require me to open up again. I don't think that my psyche could have taken being disappointed in love one more time. Time did pass, though, and I fell in love with Susan. I explained to her what life with me and Christine would be like: that I wanted to go to law school, that I could see children in my life and therefore this would be a very trying time for us. I did all I could to dissuade her from loving me and wanting to marry me. In turn, she showed me complete understanding, and a determined patience. She showed me love, true love, an acceptance of who I am that eventually gave me enough confidence to take another chance on love. I asked Susan to marry me while sitting in Hanover Park, a small park in downtown Manhattan. She said yes. Today, had she not married me and loved me the way she has, I am not sure I could have loved in marriage again or what would have become of me.

On April 22, 1979, Susan and I were married in front of one of my law school professors, a judge who was also a St. Peter's College alumnus. On July 6, 1980, my other love, Danielle was born, she made her entrance with me present in the delivery room and she was quickly placed in my arms, sighed, blew a bubble and fell asleep as tears again filled my eyes in silent conversation with her. On October 6, 1981, we were blessed with Aldo Jr. I was also there for his birth, to welcome my boy, and I knew that I just could not control the tears as he also fell asleep as soon as he was placed on my arms – seems like I am a bit boring to them.

With Danielle, Susan had a long labor over 12 hours and needed a C-Section. Danielle clocked in at 10 pounds. For Aldo, we scheduled a C-Section and all went much better for Susan; but not for me until it was all over. From what I saw and experienced, if I had been a woman, there is no way I would have allowed a man to touch me.

I started in law school in 1978, and graduated in 1983. Although Susan and I lived in the bottom apartment in her parents' house, she was completely alone with Danielle and Aldo from 7 a.m. when I left for work until about 10:30 p.m. when I returned from law school. At that time, Susan always had a hot meal for me, we would talk a bit and I would retire to study for the next day's classes until about midnight. Every other Friday I would pick Christine up, and she would spend the weekend with us. Driven by my experience with that child psychologist, I never let Christine forget that Lydia was her mom and that I was her father. To Susan and Christine's credit, they developed a very strong bond that today is very loving. One of the many things that makes Susan such a special and loving person is that she has been a mother in all possible ways a woman can be a mother. Susan was a stepmom to Christine, biological mom to Danielle and Aldo and an adoptive mom to our fourth child, Melissa. Melissa was born on September 5, 1989, and on July 27, 1990, Melissa's adoption became final. Yes, I cried again, and we became whole as a family.

***

Susan and I were bringing up a family that was increasing in size, and Susan, mostly by herself, carried us through those years. We were committed to seeing me through law school while I continued to financially support our family. Our love made it all work out.

I had applied several times for different positions at the NYSE, and had never given up in my desire to work in another department. Finally, in 1978, after graduating from college in 1977, and while I was still in law school, I was hired by Bob Flynn, a very insightful man in the NYSE Division of Market Surveillance. I worked as an analyst reviewing the trading in the stocks for possible NYSE and federal securities law violations. I was very qualified for this position and quickly started to advance. Within a year and a half I was promoted to

Investigator and Manager of our Trading Investigations Unit. Prior to being hired by Bob, I had spent almost eight years working on the trading floor of the NYSE. My duties on the trading floor included being present at the point when a buyer and a seller would meet to trade stocks on behalf of their clients and report these trades to the national "tape" for dissemination to the public.

I began to realize how and when brokers were taking advantage of each other, and I wanted to someday be able to clean things up a bit for the sake of those investors the brokers were representing. Trading violations were not rampant, but they needed to be addressed because it was difficult for those trying to enforce the rules to do this when they lacked trading knowledge. When I was hired into Market Surveillance I picked up a pattern of self-dealing that included dozens of stocks by one firm, the head of which had been the Chairman of the NYSE in the 1960s. As an analyst in Market Surveillance, I put together the package of potential violations and forwarded them to Trading Investigations for further study. The case was so large and seemed so complicated that when I was promoted to that Unit I was given that case, which I had forwarded for further review or investigation.

While I was an Investigator in Trading Investigations, a manager position was created to oversee a new trading system across the several exchanges in the United States, which had been mandated by the government. One other person applied for that position along with me. The other person was selected. I was not known as a shrinking violet, so I marched into the Director of the Department, Donald Solodar's office.

"You made a mistake by not putting me in charge of that unit. I can do a better job than the person you chose and you should know that," I told him.

"Are you finished?" he asked, smiling.

"Maybe."

"You should learn to trust people more," he said, and headed to a meeting.

Less than a month later Donald promoted me to Manager of the Trading Investigations Unit, a position I had dreamt about heading. I am not sure that I learned to trust too many others, but I learned to trust him. This was the first time in my life I had a mentor. Soon after my promotion, Donald was himself promoted to head the Floor Operations – the trading floor operations. However, our paths again crossed on two other instances, both of which were very significant in fulfilling my dreams and aspirations. I will forever be grateful to him. During that time, the stock market could not have functioned without the trading floor but there were many other divisions that made the stock market run smoothly. Today, with modern electronic trading platforms and regulations, most markets no longer need a trading floor to function. The NYSE differentiates itself in having a hybrid or combination of electronic and manual point of sale market, which necessitates a trading floor but due to its advanced electronic nature calls for a much reduced human resource requirement.

In 1981, after Donald was transferred and during an investigation of trading activity related to Spear Leeds and Kellog, the General Counsel of that firm asked me if I wanted to go to work for them. By then I was attending Seton Hall Law School. In 1980 I left the NYSE and went to work for Spear Leeds and Kellog as Assistant to the General Counsel. I wanted to have experience from the other side, the "member" trading side, and expand my knowledge of the industry.

My responsibilities included keeping an eye on the many securities-related businesses in which Spear Leeds was involved in at the time. This included an Over-the-Counter trading firm, an Options Clearing business, a

Futures Commission Merchant (FCM) clearing business, an investment advisor firm, a specialist (similar to current market makers) on the NYSE trading floor and a newly focused proprietary desk recently established by a trader, John Mulheren. Again, I applied myself the best I could and quickly gained the respect of many, as well as the knowledge of both how these businesses should work and how they really worked. I also assisted our General Counsel in legal matters, learning from him valuable lessons for future application.

John Mulheren passed away some years ago at a relatively young age; we do not have too many individuals as colorful and free spirited as John. I did not know him well but while we worked at Spear Leeds, I just, as he put it to me once, "kept him out of regulatory trouble. "John had a presence; he was loyal to friends but at one time a friend who later was found guilty of serious securities laws violations gave John's name up when questioned about those illegal trading activities. He was an incredible human being and an incredibly gifted trader. He was known to many of his friends for his propensity for pranks such as the legend of the shark – when knowing of a friend's preference for early morning swims in the pool, John allegedly had a shark placed in the pool as a companion for his swim. Another time, at a company sponsored dinner cruise in New York harbor, we waited and waited for the arrival of John and his traders. Finally, we noticed an 18th century tall ship sail toward us, and as the ship got closer and closer saw John and his traders dressed as pirates firing cannons at our ship with the purpose of boarding us. Life has to be lived and enjoyed! Every moment we breathe is a special moment. Although life is a serious journey, we should take care not to take ourselves too seriously. Life went on before we were born, and life will continue once we die; all we need to do is to make a difference while we are here.

One day, while at Spear Leeds, I learned that Donald Solodar had been promoted to Head of the Market Surveillance Division. I had heard that just before Donald's promotion, a Vice President in that Division had attempted to take his life by jumping from a 10th floor window of his office, landing on the ledge of the eighth floor cafeteria. He survived the fall. This caused the removal of the then-Head of the Division and led to Donald's promotion. During my congratulatory phone conversation to Donald, we agreed to meet for lunch. It was good to see him again; he was one of a few individuals I ever trusted, and this was the second time he would place his confidence in me and have a profound impact on my life and career.

"Aldo, I want you to come back to Market Surveillance," he said during our lunch.

"That is a very attractive concept, especially with you in charge."

"I will get you a good raise, you will be in our Special Counsel area, investigating and trying cases and I will make sure that your seniority back to when you first joined the NYSE would be recognized."

"There is no one else I would rather work for. Let me speak with Susan tonight, and I will give you my answer tomorrow," I told him.

The salary increase was exciting and needed, but the opportunity to practice and hone my legal skills and work with Donald was even more attractive. In mid-1983 I returned for my second life at the NYSE.

As soon as I arrived in Market Surveillance and reacquainted myself with friends and met new people, I was given about a half dozen cases that needed prosecution and/or settlement. I was also assigned to assist in several other cases that our Trading Investigations Unit was investigating. One of those cases involved large trading violations that I had uncovered years before as an analyst and later was assigned to me in Trading Investigations. Prior to leaving for SLK, I had concluded the investigation and had referred it to Special Counsel Unit for prosecution, and now that case was given to me to prosecute.

I was then reporting to the Chief Special Counsel, George Brunelle, a very talented attorney and great friend who reported to Agnes Gautier, the Vice President of the Department that included Special Counsel. The Chief Counsel and I had a great relationship dating back to my days as an Investigator. I had acted as his expert witness in a case of very serious violations; he had trusted my knowledge and skills, and after a day of opposing counsel cross examining me, the accused settled the case. The Chief Counsel and I both trusted each other, and all was right. I learned many things from him: strategies, tactics and work ethic. I never got over the fact that he once served a 150-page complaint on a trader on Christmas Eve. I am not sure I would have done what he did and in fact I have never done this; however, I did admire his zeal.

Not being a procrastinator, I quickly developed a plan to address and resolve my cases, and within several months had resolved all of them. The most difficult was the one I had uncovered years prior because it involved a man I admired, a former NYSE Chairman who had great vision and once negotiated the establishment of the very rule he was now accused of violating. He cried in my office the day he agreed to the settlement.

I was in my environment, utilizing all the weapons that had been formally taught to me, learned by observation and understood through experience. I had been working for 14 years, I was 33 years old, had a wonderful loving and lovable wife, incredible three children and I was starting to make my presence a factor in my career. Susan and I had come far in a short time – one step at a time, and the future lay ahead.

Chapter 10:
Commencement is Another name for Graduation

When I graduated high school and college I wondered why everyone referred to graduation as "Commencement." Well, it took graduating from law school for me to begin to understand. Commencement means "the act or time of a beginning." Without really understanding this concept, my instincts drove me to get a college and law school education. I could feel and experience my personal and professional growth as a result of learning and becoming an attorney. Truly, education was the primary moving force for the beginning of the rest of my life. Today, our graduates appear to possess not only a sense of well deserved achievement at their graduations but many exhibit a   sense of entitlement or finality: "Now that I have graduated I can do everything and should be unquestionably trusted."

My personal experience tells me otherwise. A graduate would be best served by having an approach based on the work ethic that says, "I now have what it takes to start the next level of my growth and learning, and if I work hard at learning from this life experience, I will grow to benefit others and therefore benefit myself." Self-actualization works to fine-tune the skills we need to make a difference, and then actually make a difference in the life of others. For me, graduation from college and law school reflected a stage of fine-tuning certain knowledge and skills I needed to start to make that difference.

Education is at the core of my soul. Education is the reason I have lived my dreams, and hopefully lived my imperfect life as an example to others as to what to do and not do. Education did not, and will not, prevent the rough edges of life from reaching and touching me. However, education prepared me to bring an awareness of alternatives, and how to think through and choose from those alternatives. Education provided an inner gauge to help me to realize that I can control my actions and reactions. It also facilitated my decision-making process and offered me a beginning. Education has opened doors for me, and helped me to understand that I should walk through those doors. As an attorney at the NYSE Market Surveillance Division, I started to make a difference and continued my preparation and life experience education, and this contributed to my further success.

The next challenge I faced had to do with organizational changes and constraints. Several months after I returned to Market Surveillance, the word came down that the Securities Exchange Commission (SEC) had given a not very favorable review of the Market Surveillance Exchange rules enforcement effort and, partly in response, senior management decided to move the Special Counsel Unit from the Market Surveillance Division to Enforcement. Other attorneys in the Special Counsel Unit were not pleased, and within months I was the only attorney left in that Unit as I made the move to the Enforcement Division. The only good thing was that the manager to whom I reported, Arthur Okun, was a great person, and he and I got along well immediately. However, for other reasons I was not very pleased. First, I was given all of the cases that the other attorneys in the Special Counsel Unit were handling because either no one in the Enforcement Division wanted these cases or they were not experienced in handling them.

My family on the day of my graduation from law school: Susan, Aldo Jr., Danielle and Christine.

Second, the Enforcement Division staff was not located where I had my office, at 11 Wall Street, where the individuals who developed the cases I handled were located, and where I had to take sworn testimony from traders, brokers on-the-record (OTR). Third, I had supervisors who were not familiar with the rules I had to enforce.

My first step was to tell my supervisors that I would not move blocks away to where Enforcement was located, because I had to spend most of the day where I was developing the cases: working with our analysts and investigators and conducting OTRs from all witnesses and potential rule violators. Arthur told me that his boss, the Managing Director of Enforcement, insisted I move to where they had their offices – about seven blocks away. I compromised and said, "Fine, give me an office there, and I'll keep the one I have here so I have a place to work when I am here." The Managing Director of Enforcement was a very talented attorney in his own right, but the chemistry between us never meshed very well, and truth be told, I did not help matters much.

I worked very well with Arthur and reported to him on everything I was doing, which included a large case-load – four attorneys worth of cases. A couple of weeks later Arthur said, "The Managing Director wants you here; he wants to keep a closer eye on what you do and he wants to give you some of our cases." Exasperated, I responded, "If he doesn't trust me, he can fire me – what does he think I'm doing? Besides I have timed my trips from here to there and back – each round-trip takes me 15 minutes, and if I keep going back and forth he will lose hours in a week of my productivity, in a month it will be days. You have already seen my work product – this makes no business sense, and is very burdensome on me. I will not do it, and I want you to make him see this."

Arthur responded "we should speak with him," and so the next day we met at his office to discuss one of the cases in which we had a difference of opinion as to how to proceed. As the Managing Director visibly became upset, partly due to my behavior, I noticed that he reached for a dish on his desk, picked up what I thought to be candy, and after a few minutes as he swished them in his mouth he abruptly took them out and placed them back on the dish. They were pebbles! "Rocks!" I screamed inside – "Rocks!"

Arthur and I looked at each other. Arthur had the look that said, "Now you know what I know." I quickly ended the meeting, and while leaving the office with Arthur, whispered to him, "I will not drive myself into the ground for someone who sucks rocks!"

Maybe this was not the best approach, but I was not very much bothered after that. Another year passed under these tenuous conditions, and when I least expected it, I was again pressured to move to Enforcements' offices.

Enforcement Division implemented a time-tracking device that was, in my opinion, unduly burdensome to me and useless from a point of view of informing supervisors of the progress of our cases. It was easy to manipulate to account for time spent working on cases.

Sometime just before my second anniversary at Enforcement I had to undergo my annual performance review, and although I had tried or settled over two dozen cases, conducted over 65 OTRs and assisted Market Surveillance staff in preparing cases in over 35 other items, I received a "meets requirement" instead of "exceeds" or "outstanding." In addition, in that review I was asked, as my next year's goal, to almost double my performance. I was extremely disappointed and wondered what the agenda was in insisting on these performance measures. Although I was unable to alter much of this review, this was the first of only two occasions when I objected and commented on my performance review. However, never did I decide to lessen my commitment to the work, the position or to others. On the contrary, I stepped up. I have seen individuals who, when faced with people who do not believe in them, give up or reduce their efforts. I learned that to do so is self-destructive. If I had given up, I would have played into the hands of whoever did not want to see me succeed. I learned to reinvigorate my commitment and prove that person wrong. Coincidentally, just as my performance review was finalized, another SEC review came down noting that during the last two years, NYSE had experienced the most productive enforcement period, bringing more cases than in any prior two-year period. I felt completely vindicated, since

My brother, Migue on my law school graduation day.

I was the only attorney assigned to those cases. The SEC was unknowingly recognizing my efforts. In October 1985, a position of Director of Regulatory Quality Review (RQR) became vacant. I applied and got the position. Soon after I accepted that position, I learned that the SEC review that favorably commented on the contribution I made had also found that the Enforcement Division had its problems and that the rock-sucking managing director had left the NYSE. As the Director of RQR, I now had responsibility to review and make recommendations about the adequacy of

Market Surveillance procedures and whether those procedures were effective or if changes should be made. RQR was the regulatory quality assurance process, and this meant that I was now in a position to again make a difference by working to identify problems and correct them before they became significant issues.

For the first time, I had a staff to manage, and once again I was ready and confident to tackle a new challenge. I was learning some very important lessons. I enjoyed the opportunity to put into practice and experience some of what I had learned in college about management skills. Also, my duties called for reviewing and "recommending." Since I did not have authority to effect change, just to recommend change, an entire realm of possibilities opened up to me. I faced the opportunity to expand and master entirely different skills. I reached out and suddenly became responsible for the performance of others and to observe, analyze and interpret better ways to perform a function. I realized that caring was a characteristic not new to me. I cared very much for my family, and when we care we look into the future, and I was very comfortable with that thought. Also, since trust is the prime mover in all relationships, I realized that in order to be trusted by those reporting to me and by those to whom I would be recommending changes, I needed to be honest and fair in the way I dealt with them. Years later I knew that being honest and fair with those I was responsible for and having a vision that I could communicate is what leadership is all about. It is how a leader is trusted and indicates the leader cares about those under him.

From 1985 until 1987, I experimented with this leadership concept by trial and error. I believe I was more effective in pinpointing what needed to be changed and how to change it than with my management capabilities, but I was improving as I went along. I struggled with making others see the changes that needed to be made. However, something was happening that would prove I was headed in the right direction, and it had to do with the insider trading scandals in Wall Street in the mid-1980s. The industry regulators such as the NYSE and SEC had failed to uncover a massive insider trading scandal where traders, members of the NYSE and employees of NYSE member firms were illegally obtaining and paying for material: nonpublic information regarding publicly traded companies, and trading favorably ahead of the publication of such events, illegally profiting in huge sums.

The NYSE in October 1987 decided to expand its then current efforts to address and enhance detection of potential trading violations and create an additional 20-plus department – Market Trading Analysis II – in order to address this systemic breakdown in detection and investigation of potential insider trading and market manipulation. Donald Solodar, who at this time was heading Market Surveillance Division, for the third time put his trust in me and offered me the promotion to Managing Director, heading this new Department. As he put it, "I want you to work together with Agnes...and fix it." Agnes Gautier was the Vice President of Market Trading Analysis I, a person I held in high regard and looked forward to working with. Four years earlier, in 1984, I had worked for her when Donald brought me back to the NYSE into the Special Counsel Unit. Two years later, in 1989, Bob McSweeney, the new Head of the Division, promoted me to Vice President. Working together, our success was palpable. Within three years we had turned the situation around and were in the process of designing and developing the most sophisticated electronics and systems to detect, investigate and gather evidence of insider trading and other trading abuses.

In 1987, I became the first Hispanic Managing

Director at the NYSE, and two years later the only Hispanic Vice President of the NYSE and at 39 years old, one of the youngest. This was further confirmation that my parents' sacrifice and unspoken gift to me, in sending me to the United States in 1962, was working as they intended – I was living my dream. It also did not go unnoticed by me that I had already been working for 20 years, since 1969. It had taken me 18 to 20 years to get this far, and I was so young. I was making a difference in the lives of those for whose performance I was responsible. I was making a difference to investors who relied on our regulatory brand to maintain fair and orderly markets. I was making a difference in the reputation of the NYSE as a market of high integrity and concern for the interests of investors around the world, and consequently I was making a difference in the lives of Susan and our children. I was living the example I hoped they would understand. Although I took the longer path to my education: six years at night for college instead of four, and four and a half years at night for law school instead of three, my efforts and Susan's sacrifices had led us to this point. I was 38, and she was 33 – life moves quickly at times, and if we take the right steps we will be ready for it. We grew up fast.

Professionally and at home, 1983 to 1989 were very successful years, yet life always keeps us level-headed and grounded. In September 1985, Susan, Danielle, Aldo and I moved from North Plainfield, New Jersey to Hillsborough, New Jersey. We made this move and had our home built because Danielle and Aldo would soon be entering school, and we wanted to provide them with quality academic and religious education and the stability to make and keep friends. We wanted to put down roots. While in North Plainfield, Susan had become involved in the Junior Women's League and established a food bank and worked to address community issues. Our life was changing right in front of our eyes, and we enjoyed discussing the changes and the direction we were headed. We were on our journey. We were putting in the time, working hard and enjoying life and each other.

That is not to say that we had not encountered obstacles. Susan was very close to her dad, and he fell very ill from a brain tumor and in 1984 passed away. This hit us very hard, especially Susan. He was young, 59, and strong, and his death reminded us that we don't have each other forever on this earth and love should be present in our minds every day of our lives. Life, like all things beautiful, is very fragile, and we must treasure our loved ones every day for as long as we can.

I never had the chance to share with my parents the fruit of their sacrifice and their gift to me. I was given news of my promotion to Managing Director, Department Head, October 6, 1987. My father went into the hospital with high fevers and difficulty in breathing in early September 1987. My mom, at age 56, died a few days later, on September 10. Then my dad died on October 5, two months before his 62nd birthday and a day before I was told about my promotion.

My mom had struggled for a long time with a debilitating heart condition, emotional problems going back to her childhood and depression that became very difficult to control at that time. In early 1987, she and my brother, Migue, moved in with us because Migue had years earlier been hit hard by the loss of his dad. My mom had also divorced my brother's dad. In 1987, my brother was a college student living in the dorm at Rutgers University. On that morning in September I got up as usual and went to work. A short time after I arrived, Susan called me.

"Mom is dead," she told me when I answered the phone.

I was speechless, cold. I wasn't sure I was breathing.

"Come home, your mom committed suicide. I found her in her room. She didn't answer when I called. She was kneeling."

Death comes as quickly as life, but in birth we have time, we expect it and we prepare for it. With death, we don't have that certainty of when it will happen, and often death does not give us time to prepare to receive it. I felt weak; my mom was no longer around for us – my relationship with her was over. My emotions fought each other. The thought that "I will not have her anymore" warred with the thought, "how could she do this?" That made me angry. I have always regarded suicide, and still do, as an act of cowardice. However, I have had time to understand that one must be aware of conditions that take over our ability to reason in a healthy manner. When this happens, very unimaginable alternatives can result; such was my mom's condition.

I was experiencing all of these thoughts and emotions even while I was still on the telephone with Susan. I also knew that my next task was to let my brother know what had happened. "How will he take it? How do I tell him?" I wondered. I knew I had to tell him in person. Migue was only 18 years old, and he had just lost his second parent. I worried about him.

The words "Mom is dead – she committed suicide" repeated themselves in my head.

It was only a few days earlier that my dad had been hospitalized, and he had said to me, "Be careful with your mom; she is not well." I knew that, but had not understood. My dad always cared for my mom, and even though they never reunited, they had a special relationship and they spoke with each other from time to time.

A few days later, the day of my mom's wake, I was told by dad's doctor that he had a type of pneumonia caused by the HIV virus. In 1984, after his mother died, my dad had entered into many questionable relations with a number of women. Throwing oneself to reckless abandon is also a way of giving up. When I tried to talk to him about his new lifestyle, he refused to address the subject with me. By the time he went to the hospital the disease was well established; he was intubated the day he told me to watch out for mom and quickly needed a respirator. Before he was intubated, however, he asked me to bring him a priest. He was extremely restless and needed to confess. After the priest gave him his last rites and forgave him for his actions, my dad completely changed. He seemed at peace and resigned about his destiny. Seeing him in this acceptance made me more accepting as well – death is not to be feared; it is part of life but we need to be ready to accept it. The day after that he was placed on a respirator and quickly fell into a coma. Of course, I had told this to my mom.

The day after mom died I went to visit Dad as I did almost every day until he died on October 10. As I sat there with him, holding his hand, I said to him, "Mom died yesterday." His eyelids fluttered for a second or two; it was the only reaction I saw from him after he went into the coma.

I had many one-sided conversations with Dad while he was in that coma. I kept pushing the doctors to shut the respirator off and allow him to move on. Finally, the doctors agreed with me, and we set October 6 as the day the respirator would be shut down. My dad died hours before that was to happen.

What we faced as a family was not only unexpected, but severe. Even though I had been worried about my mom's state of mind, I had not seen any of this coming. My emotions ranged from guilt to anger at both of my parents – at my mom because I thought of suicide as a cowardly act, and I had never thought my mom as a coward. But I came to believe she did this for us as well.

She understood she had problems, and at times she got into arguments with us that she knew she should not have. She left a note saying she was sorry, and expanded on things that betrayed her inner struggles and lack of reasoning in a capable manner. Suicide is never a rational action.

There were things I wanted to say to both of my parents that were never said. I will never again hold back anything I want to say to someone I love. I think I am saddest that they never got to see the fruit of their sacrifice in sending me out of Cuba, because they did not live long enough to know about my success at the NYSE – and they both came so close. "If only they had lived a few more days," I thought. I felt devastated, as if I had been punched and beaten for 25 days straight.

Susan and I found strength in each other. We focused on the children, in making sure that we explained the situation to all of them, Christine, Danielle and Aldo, the best we could, as accurately as we could, to satisfy their questions and concerns.

We were very worried about my brother; he was almost 19 years old but I did not think of him as that age. He needed his time; we made sure we were there for him whenever he needed us. However, my brother showed us a strength of character, a search for the meaning of his life. He was an Eagle Scout and always had a loving and good heart, but after losing his dad and then mom, he called upon all the strength within him to come through his trial and persevere in still traveling a successful journey with his loving wife, Toni Ann, who has given him the love and strength that those who belong together can only give to each other. My brother is one of those people I greatly admire; he fought and fought through all of this and went through his trials by fire. Today he is a trusted doctor and loving husband, greatly loved by his wife who stood by him through the very long process to become a doctor.

During those very dark days of October 1987, Susan and I decided that the only thing that was going to get the family through this challenge was to rely solely on our love for each other, just as life had shown to both of us so many times before. We did, and although I don't remember when, we started to look back and laugh at the good memories of my parents, their silly habits and behavior. We realized that the healing process was well on its way. Life is not easy, and that is fine.

***

Heading back to work, only a couple of days into my new position, the market crash of October 1987 hit and panic struck the investing world for several days before confidence was restored – what a way to start a new job! I was responsible for more than 20 professionals whose job was to try to catch individuals violating securities laws, particularly those engaged in insider trading and market manipulation, a process I knew had to be fixed. At the same time I also had new employees to be hired and emotional family conditions. Love is the greatest gift of all. As I have said before, I am not overtly religious, but I am spiritual, and I believe in the life example of Jesus Christ, love personified. All I could do was to bring that love and caring along with trust in my own capabilities with me as I set off into the future. I set short and simple objectives and let the confidence build again in me and in others.

As I tried to make sense of all that took place in September and October 1987, I knew that I wanted to give back to others in the name of my parents. At the end of October, I volunteered to go into the classrooms in New York City to work with Junior Achievement. I was able to arrange my schedule at work to permit me one class a week for a couple of hours from September to May.

Chapter 11:
The Burdens of Leadership

A leader has the responsibility for tomorrow. A leader is responsible for having the vision of where he wants to take us. A leader has the responsibility to muster the current resources available to take us there. A leader must use his mind and inspire us, caring for us so we can trust in that leadership. A leader cannot afford the luxury to use his heart without first checking his mind to insure he has our best interest in mind. My entire life experience can be encapsulated in the events of September 11, 2001, and the developments that would follow this evil date. The events and lessons touched all of us in one way or another, and for some that impact will for the rest of our lives; 9/11 is a day that will forever be a part of us, engraved in our hearts and minds. It is a day of great experiences and revelations that, once again, put my life in perspective.

That Tuesday began the same as any other day. In my home, the radio alarm rang at 6 a.m., Susan shut it off and made sure that I was up – I have always been a night owl and moving up and out of bed is the toughest part of my day. I grunted to prove that I was awake, turned to her and, as I always did, gave her a hug, got up and showered. As I dressed, Susan, as always, had the TV on to check on the weather and news. At 6:45 a.m., I kissed her, told her I loved her and went to work, driving about seven miles to my train station in Raritan. On the way, as always, I stopped to get coffee, a cream cheese bagel, the Wall Street Journal and New York Times. I took the usual 7:13 a.m. express train from Raritan to Newark, and met my usual commuting friends in the train. We briefly chatted, talked about baseball – the season was nearing its end – and talked about football – the season was brand new.

The trip into Newark Penn Station took roughly an hour, so at about 8:15 a.m. we arrived in Newark and went our separate ways. I hopped in the Path train that took me to the World Trade Center, the end of the line, and as always, unless I came in early for a meeting, by about 8:40 a.m., I arrived at the lowest level of the Trade Center. At about 8:45 a.m., I surfaced to the street to walk to the NYSE about five blocks away.

As I came out of the building the first thing that hit me was what an extremely beautiful day it was; bright blue sky, gentle, cooling breeze, no humidity, and as I looked up, the two towers mapped against the cloudless blue sky looked so majestic and so miraculous, a simple and soft prayer spilled from my lips – "Thank you, Lord for such a beautiful day." I continued walking to work thinking, "In 1969 when I started to work here, you (the towers) were not completed yet – you're looking good."

On that morning my senses seemed particularly heightened. I noticed everything; people looked happy, they walked with a hop in their steps. Taxi cabs did not seem as aggressive as usual, and tourists were not in the way. As I arrived at the NYSE, I noticed – couldn't miss it – a huge truck, part of a digging effort, right outside the building at 11 Wall Street. I greeted our guards at the door and took the elevator to my office.

Less than 10 minutes after saying my simple prayer of thanks, I stepped from the elevator on the 10th floor where I had my office and heard a sudden loud noise followed by the building shaking, hard. For a short second I paused. "Maybe the truck fell into the hole outside or maybe it's an earthquake," I thought, and quickly walked to our "Stock Watch" area to see if I could find out what had happened. From Stock Watch, our analysts monitored in real time what was taking place in our market. Stock Watch had the latest news feed and was staffed early every day.

"What was that? Do we know what happened?" I asked.

"We don't know, but we're hearing a plane crashed into the World Trade Center," they said.

"Thanks, I'll be back," I said and went to my office to leave my briefcase and quickly return to Stock Watch.

"They're confirming it was a plane, but there is no more information yet," one of the analysts said as I arrived back at the desk.

"This does not look good. What kind of plane was it?"

I was thinking that unless it was a small plane and the noise and tremor did not indicate that it was, it could be an act of terrorism. The sky had been too clear; there was not a cloud to be seen. I didn't think a large jet could have accidentally crashed against the building in such clear conditions. I went back to my office to call Susan and let her know something had happened at the World Trade Center and that I was fine. I then took a walk around our floor and checked to see who in my department was in already and who was not.

As I walked around I stopped in at Stock Watch again and learned a passenger jet plane had crashed into one of the towers. As I stood there, a second loud noise and another tremor shook our building – the second plane had flown into the other tower. We were under attack, and no one needed to say it. I went back and called Susan again. "Turn on your cell phone, the computer, everything; call Aldo, and Brian (our son-in-law) and tell them to get away from Manhattan," I told her.

At the time Aldo was a student at Pratt Institute in Manhattan and Brian worked on 38th street – my worry was that the Empire State Building might be the next target, and if so, they would be caught in the midst of that disaster. I couldn't afford to worry about them, I needed to account and care for my people, my department and my friends. I kept thinking about the thousands of people who were in those towers. The NYSE had a division, more than 100 people in one of the towers, and everyone worried. It would be an hour and a half before I would again speak with Susan. We all just took one step in front of the other; we were only in control of our reactions to each moment as it happened.

I needed to know where my colleagues were, not everyone had arrived at work, and slowly we began accounting for each other. Eventually we learned that every one of our folks in our department was accounted for and that everyone who worked in one of the Twin Towers was safe. After the 1993 bombing of the World Trade Center our team had been instructed to leave the building at the first sign of trouble, and they had listened well. We were also fortunate to have had a clinic in our building. It quickly filled to capacity, and the staff of doctors and nurses worked tirelessly and selflessly in attending to everyone – thankfully no one was seriously hurt, although there were some injuries. One individual had just gotten off the bus two blocks away when the second plane hit, and as fiery debris fell in all directions around her, she feared for her life. My worry remained with my son and son-in-law and where the next plane would strike. Suddenly our media outlets in Stock Watch announced that the Pentagon had been struck – more tragedy, but by now expected. However, notwithstanding the loss of life in Washington, DC, for the second time that day I breathed a sigh of relief. The terrorists had finished with New York, I thought, and my son and son-in-law would be safe.

Security told everyone in the building to evacuate to the trading floor. It had been retrofitted for high security conditions with its own air ventilation system and air-tight facilities. The people in our department started the descent to the ground floor from the 10th floor via what was considered an outside staircase even though it was enclosed, all concrete with no windows. As most of the staff headed down, a couple of other individuals and I checked to make sure that no one had remained behind on that floor. As I left one of the offices, I turned to look out one of the windows that surrounded our workplace. Suddenly, a sustained and horrifying noise, followed by a totally consuming dark cloud of smoke and debris, approached our building. I watched as the cloud engulfed us. For a few seconds I stood motionless with a few others just watching. A new fear struck me, one that I have never felt before, not even in my loneliest hours: I had no way of knowing what was behind that cloud. I realized that one of the towers must have collapsed. Finally, we turned from the windows and proceeded quickly to the staircase and evacuated the floor. For the sake of the others on the staircase, I could not show my fear or cause panic. We were oganized and were moving down as quickly and smoothly as possible. "A department head must remain calm" I insisted to myself.

While the cloud that I had watched seemed to envelop our building completely, no ash or smoke rushed inward at that time. Eventually, the ash would to some extent invade the building.

We congregated in the trading floor at the lobby of 11 Wall Street and waited, checked on each other and tried to ascertain what had happened and what was happening. As time passed, the second tower fell – this time we knew what was happening. I walked past a location where some people had gathered to watch TV and see what was taking place just five blocks away. As I stood there and watched the fallen towers I was stricken, almost paralyzed, thinking about what Susan at home was watching. The view on the television screen showed that dark smoke that had overcome our building had moved over the entire southern tip of lower Manhattan, as if the towers had collapsed over the entire area.

"Susan! I have to tell her I am alive," I screamed inside of myself, and immediately asked someone from one of the firms on the trading floor to let me make an outside call. Finally, after about an hour and a half since I had last spoken with her, I was able to bring her some peace that I was alive. She told me that Brian was safe across the river in Jersey and Aldo was trying to get to me downtown, but the police would not allow any one south of Canal Street – the best news of the day! Susan mentioned that phone calls were pouring in at home from everywhere, Texas, Spain, Cuba. I would later have to return 21 phone calls from friends and relatives, not including those who lived close by and who came to our home to find out how we were.

By about 1:15 p.m., there had been no further

occurrences, and as conditions appeared calm, we were told that it would be best to attempt to leave the building and head home. We would be told when to return to work. The entire capability of opening the NYSE for business had been destroyed. Anger had settled in by now; not just for me, but for everyone there. We could see it grow in each others' eyes. Thousands had been slaughtered at the World Trade Center, and they included innocents from all over the world – this evil represented the worst of mankind.

But, no matter how angry we were, our next step was to head out for home. I checked with the other people in our department and learned that everyone had already made a plan to get home.

A group of us decided to exit the Broad Street side of the building and head east away from the fires and dark smoke coming from where the Twin Towers had stood just two hours before. Our plan was to turn left and then walk north until we could get to midtown Manhattan. As we stepped outside, that beautiful exhilarating day we had all woken up to was in the distant past – the color gray was dominant. The scene could have been a re-creation from a science fiction movie about a nuclear holocaust. About a quarter of an inch of gray ash covered the sidewalks, streets, buildings, building ledges, roofs, cars, fire trucks, police, firemen and people who were not as lucky as we had been and had been caught outside. We walked on streets that were lifeless except for others who were trudging out of the city, just like we were. As planned, we headed east to Water Street and just before we turned left, north, we spotted a large crowd where regularly the ferry docked, and decided to see if the ferries were operating – not only were they operating, but what we saw was incomprehensible.

Hundreds, maybe thousands, of vessels and boats of all kinds, privately owned and otherwise, were docking to take anyone, all of us in downtown Manhattan, to safety in New Jersey. People were more than helpful; they were anxious to come to our rescue and ferry us to safety. I have read about the great boatlift at Dunkirk in Europe at the start of World War II, when thousands of British and French troops were rescued from the coast of France and taken to England in small boats, and I thought to myself, "This is what it must have looked like."

A short time later, sitting in a ferry crossing New York Harbor and passing by where the Twin Towers had stood just that morning, the air was black and heavy; inextinguishable fire and smoke that billowed south into the sea. I angrily prayed in silence, only my lips moving, knowing that thousands had died. It was an incredible weight to carry that day. About an hour later, trousers covered in ash, I stood with a group of others from the ferry as we arrived at Newark Penn Station where police were offering to hose us down to clean the ash from our clothes. I took the train back to Raritan, called Susan and told her I was coming home. Later I learned that Danielle, our second oldest who was attending Lehigh University in Pennsylvania, had been beside herself, even though she and Susan had been in touch often throughout the day. Danielle, who was working as a summer intern at the NYSE, knew exactly where the events were taking place and, of course, many of the people who worked there. Luckily, by the time I arrived back in New Jersey, Melissa, our youngest, who was in seventh grade at St. Ann School, was no longer worried. She had been told in school that I was fine and coming back home.

The next day, sitting at home 50 miles or so away from Manhattan, the winds shifted a bit, and I could smell the fires from the World Trade Center. By now the world knew who was responsible for this cowardly and inhuman act, and anger had set in. At that moment, this anger fed a determination that had many of us who worked in lower Manhattan and at the NYSE asking, "What can we do when we get back to work?" The only thing we could do was to return to our daily lives, to our work, and show the world that we were not defeated, that we were committed to honoring those souls lost and all of those families affected by getting back to doing what they had lived and fought and died to do. We didn't know how long it would be – how long before we could show the world and these lifeless individuals the real strength of America?

Before the NYSE opened for business again on September 17, 2001, a good number of people had to work round-the-clock to rebuild the electronic infrastructure that had been totally destroyed, including our member firms' capabilities that enabled them to connect with the order routing and execution systems of the NYSE. But we were back that next week – incredible comeback. As we returned to work the fires remained burning, and we could smell them. Small amounts of ashes were visible on papers on our desks. When I arrived back at my office on that day, I had a call from the staff of the SEC. I returned the call; we were back in business, and we knew what we had to do. As days passed we learned of friends who had died there and friends who but for unexpected quirks were not inside the World Trade Center Towers that day and lived – inexplicable occurrences.

In the aftermath of that day, we came together as a people, we died together, we lost friends and family members together and we remained in life together. Our families' structures strengthened, and our love for each other was palpable.

But that feeling did not last; our leaders strayed and took political advantage and sent us to war – why? Against whom? Our nation lost a great opportunity to grow, and our leaders resorted to divisive behaviors.

Our government took action based on inaccurate information, and we gave medals to those who were responsible for providing us with information – why was there no accountability? We sent thousands to their deaths as we relied on that inaccurate information – why? What has 9/11 taught us? For me, it showed our great capacity to love, to sacrifice, to rebuild, to recommit, the strength of family. But it also disclosed a great weakness: our emphasis on using our hearts at the risk of excluding our minds when we make decisions.

Conclusion: Milestones and Next Steps

Ask yourself, "Do I have a passion? Do I have an image, a vision of who I want to be? What I want to do and how I want to do it?" If the answer is "yes," then work toward that passion; go and do it, make it happen. If the answer is "no," and you feel bored, then dare to dream, dare to face your fears, particularly your fears of failing. Don't hesitate. Because you will not be satisfied; you will not experience the joy and peace of happiness unless you conquer your fears; unless you find your passion; unless you overcome your obstacles and challenges and step through those bars that appear to protect you, but in reality hold you back – unless you give in to love.

My story is a story of failures, successes, dysfunction, loneliness, desperation and love – and so is your story.

We just need to know that we have more control over our destiny than we think we do. My dream did not materialize on a day's notice. I was not born wanting to be a doctor or a mechanic, or work at the NYSE. I did not sit down one day and say to myself, here is what I want to do.

But I thought about it, often and a little at a time, beginning as a teenager and lasting through adulthood.

Susan and me with our daughter Melissa at her graduation

As I thought about it I came to have answers to these questions, and you will, too – be patient but persevere, don't give up – you just might have several dreams.

Life is a beautiful journey. We can see our physical growth but it is more difficult to realize our personal, spiritual and psychological growth, which an education that develops our critical and analytical thinking, along with life experience, provides. Do not fear the unknown. I have learned that life is not so much about whether we fail or triumph, but about how we react when we fail and triumph. So experience the moment – the failures and successes; learn from them.

Today, looking back, I can point to certain eye-opening or watershed times in my life. Certainly, in 1957 when at seven years old, I became the child of a dysfunctional family with my parents' divorce. Two years later, I came face to face with violence, death and killing in the streets of La Habana. Leaving my parents and my native country in 1962 for a life of utter uncertainty changed me and helped me to learn to assert myself and handle loneliness and disappointment. These events helped me to realize that I could deal with a lot more than I thought I was capable of. High school graduation and starting to work full time in 1969 was the year when I turned my life into a major thoroughfare and chose a path to follow. I lump together the births of each of my children and my daughter Melissa's arrival, because each time I held those babies for the first time my heart experienced the joy of life. The year of 1987 was a mixture of pain and jubilation I pray not to experience again, but it also represented the year I decided to start giving back to the community, volunteering to work with Junior Achievement of New York and to go into the classrooms in New York and New Jersey to teach a financial literacy course to elementary and high school students. I never stopped participating in this activity until I retired from the NYSE in 2008, 21 years later. From 2006 to 2008, I served on the Board of the Directors of Junior Achievement of New York (JANY), representing the NYSE. Education has been the key to my success, and I am dedicated to making the experience as productive, constructive and pleasant for the students as I can.

At work, since 1987, many of us from different departments successfully worked together – after some early rough going – to develop both the systems and the professional staff needed to address the challenges of bringing technology to the NYSE. I remained in this area for many years, building on successes to develop a reliant and trusting working relationship with government regulators, all regulatory staff and among all market regulators in the United States and abroad. I re-presented the NYSE for years in a network of more than

50 exchanges and markets across the world, and in 2006 had the privilege of serving as the Chair of that network. During that time, we were able to expand our cooperation capabilities across these markets to improve our capabilities to meet our individual regulatory responsibilities and improve the chances of catching, across national boundaries, those who violated the securities laws of our respective jurisdictions. I became familiar with the ugly side of greed, discovering that greed knows no limitation; some wealthy individuals would violate the law for small and insignificant sums of money, almost as often, it seemed, as those who schemed to illegally profit in large sums at the expense of others. I also came to realize that some of those individuals were not adequately informed that their conduct was illegal – individuals and families were at times destroyed because people were just unaware that what they were doing was illegal! Educating ourselves – becoming knowledgeable of the possibilities and of our responsibilities – can often be a true deterrent to self-destruction.

In 2004, I was moved to another department by Robert Marchman, another senior executive I respected and to whom I reported for three years. This new department was put together as a result of a divisional reorganization, and I was given different and additional responsibilities regarding options trading surveillance and public investor concerns. Other added responsibilities included coordinating the Market Surveillance options surveillance integration from another exchange that the NYSE acquired. I was also tasked to coordinate a committee that reviewed new products to be listed for trading at the NYSE, and I was asked to serve on a review committee to evaluate applications from companies that desired to list at the NYSE for trading.

Throughout all these years, I wanted to be as involved with my children as possible. For twelve years I coached Danielle and Aldo in CYO basketball, and when there was no girls' team at Danielle's school, we started one. After Danielle went to high school, where she played varsity ball, we started a CYO high school boys' team, and I coached while Aldo Jr. was involved. I have learned so much from so many people, including my children, and I hope that, in turn, I have been an example to them with respect to what they may choose to do and not do; that they understand that while no one is ever perfect or wins every time, the important thing is to stick your neck out, try, get involved, and be part of life.

And I have kept giving back; while at the NYSE, I also served as Chair of St. Athanasius School, an elementary school in The Bronx that was threatened with closure about ten years ago. It survived after several people assisted in prioritizing its needs and finances and worked to create an environment for the

Sitting in the backyard with Susan, Spring, 2012

school to grow and improve academically by making it possible for donors to contribute to its revitalization. While Melissa attended high school, Susan and I served on that school's Development Cabinet for four years, the last one as co-chairs of the Cabinet.

I retired in March 2008 from the NYSE to continue on my journey. I still concentrate on education, no surprise there – I serve on the Board of Regents of St. Peter's College where I am also adjunct professor of Derivative Markets, Corporate Finance and Investment Analysis in the MBA program. I am the president of the St. Ann School Advisory Council in Raritan, New Jersey, the elementary school where Danielle, Aldo and Melissa attended. I have served on corporate boards and presently serve on the Board of the Capital Markets Research Cooperative Center in Australia, a joint venture between academia and government. In 2011, I unsuccessfully ran for office for the Hillsborough Township Committee because I was not pleased with the way our Township Committee is governing. As these last few lines are written, I find myself running for my town's School Board – still driven to serve in areas I am confident I can make a difference.

Tomorrow, after this book is written, what will I do? Who knows? I have been giving back for quite some time, and I do not see that stopping. I am pleased in the difference I have made in the lives of others, and what truly energizes me is that others have benefitted by my actions without really having been aware of my actions. My journey continues; my purpose to serve and make a difference is what drives me. I have learned to trust my instincts and that if I take the right steps, life will be okay.

Those ornate bars from my early childhood memories are no longer needed to either protect me or to keep me from reaching out. To the day I die, I will be mindful and thankful for the greatest unspoken gift my mom and dad gave to me – their sacrifice of sending me to my country of choice so that I could become the person I wanted to be. They gifted me that opportunity with unconditional love, even knowing it might mean that they would never to see me again. I am imperfect – I accept that – but having experienced such gift, I respect their honorable lives by doing the best I can to make a difference – knowing this, I look forward to tomorrow's challenges. My life has been, and will continue to be, imperfect, but my motivation for living is focused on making a difference in the well-being of others – shouldn't that be enough?

Acknowledgement

The lines that follow would never have been written but for the patient and insightful dedication of Karen Miller. Karen, you not only coached me and pushed me to face my past but made me dig deep into my soul for the feelings that my memory deciphered. You knew how significant those feelings were to me and to those who may be helped by this experience and explained to me how to express them.

I will always be grateful to you for guiding me in this therapeutic and rejuvenating journey.

About the Author

As you read The Unspoken Gift, you have come to understand the setting for Aldo Martinez' success in life and in his career with the New York Stock Exchange. The intimate portrayal of his early experiences set  the path for a commitment to family and community that continues through today. For close to 40 years, Martinez worked at the New York Stock Exchange, first on the trading floor, and then in regulatory and legal matters. While at the NYSE, he headed two departments tasked with developing surveillance criteria and investigation of potential illegal insider trading, market manipulation, frontrunning and other trading abuses in equities and derivatives. He became the first Hispanic to rise to the level of Vice President at the NYSE.

Martinez' high ethical integrity, extensive knowledge and interpersonal abilities have led him to develop a respectful and caring attitude for those with whom he works, resulting in their individual professional development including facilitating divisional NYSE training programs and other training opportunities. Internationally, Martinez has worked to expand the reaches and strengthen the cooperative ties among in Jersey City, New Jersey, where he received his bachelor's degree in business administration, and now teaches Derivative Markets, Corporate Finance and Investment Analysis at St. Peter's University.

Martinez has served on a number of corporate boards and has been involved in a wide variety of community activities, including serving on the Board of Regents of St. Peter's University in Jersey City, New Jersey and on boards of several advisory school councils as well as having worked with Junior Achievement of New York. His family continues to support him by encouraging and insisting that The Unspoken Gift be shared with many.

CPSIA information can be obtained at www.ICGtesting.com
Printed in the USA
LVOW070902041012

301321LV00003BC/98/P